My Road to Paradise

*Paradise, a place where hopes
and dreams gather to meet
with uncommon reality.*

FRANK PHILLIPS

WESTBOW
P R E S S®
A DIVISION OF THOMAS NELSON
& ZONDERVAN

WestBow Press books may be ordered through booksellers or by contacting:

WestBow Press
A Division of Thomas Nelson & Zondervan
1663 Liberty Drive
Bloomington, IN 47403
www.westbowpress.com
1 (866) 928-1240

ISBN: 978-1-9736-6289-1 (sc)
ISBN: 978-1-9736-6290-7 (hc)
ISBN: 978-1-9736-6288-4 (e)

Library of Congress Control Number: 2019907151

Print information available on the last page.

WestBow Press rev. date: 6/11/2019

Contents

Acknowledgments vii

Introduction ix

CHAPTER 1   The Family Circle 1

CHAPTER 2   The Table 9

CHAPTER 3   The Road 19

CHAPTER 4   The Blender 27

CHAPTER 5   The Bible 35

CHAPTER 6   The Father 45

CHAPTER 7   The Son 53

CHAPTER 8   The Holy Spirit 65

CHAPTER 9   The Tree of Knowledge 75

CHAPTER 10   The Wine Glasses 85

CHAPTER 11   The One-Dollar Bill 93

CHAPTER 12   The Beautician 101

CHAPTER 13   The Last Mile 109

Epilogue 117

Acknowledgments

I know of no better way to acknowledge the time and effort my wife devoted to *My Road to Paradise* than to quote the words Christ spoke to His Father: "I have completed the work You gave me to do." Sandy, you contributed so much more than I asked. Your review and editorial skills are exceeded only by your passion for Christ and family. Thank you for your love of Christ; it warms the rooms of our home. Thank you for the laughter that echoes throughout and for the open door that always welcomes our guests.

To the Wednesday-morning Bible study group at the BRCC. Your love for Christ and the words of wisdom that are shared each week are truly inspiring. Thank you for allowing me to be part of your lives.

Then there is GLF, a church where the love of Jesus Christ and God's grace are a way of life. Thank you for being a lamp to my feet and a light that helps to guide me along *My Road to Paradise*.

Finally, thank You, Lord, for showing me the way, truth, and life; and for silhouetting the holy hills of heaven with Your everlasting light, a light that will eventually lead me home to my new address in paradise.

Introduction

As a child growing up, my dreams of paradise were never more than an idle thought away. These imaginary places offered me the opportunity to step from a world of reality, cross its border, and go into my own concept of paradise. It was a world filled with mythical places, dressed with unimaginable beauty, and overpopulated with wonderful opportunities; all of them came with unlimited resources. My plans were to leave home as soon as possible and to go in search of this imaginary place, so upon graduation from high school, I enlisted in the US Army. I quickly realized the stuff dreams are made of doesn't necessarily translate into even the most rudimentary facts of life, especially when you are looking from the deck of a troop carrier ship. Instead of paradise, I saw Inchon Harbor, Korea, my new home for the next fourteen months.

A few weeks after arriving in Korea, I enrolled in a parachute-rigging class. A group of army parachute riggers taught the class. After some pretty intensive training, the sergeant in charge of the program came up to me one evening and gave me a chute, told me to pack it, and said tomorrow I would have the privilege of jumping with it strapped to my back. The next morning we loaded our parachutes and other equipment onto the back of a three-quarter-ton truck and headed to Camp Casey, where the drop zone was located. It was really cold outside, but it was warm and comfy riding in the cab of this canvas-topped truck with the three other soldiers in my group. My thoughts centered on, *Today is really going to be a good day.*

We jumped from two thousand feet. Since my parachute, the one I had personally packed, opened, I counted it a "double-good day." But a gust of wind carried me away from the drop zone, and although I had limited control over my direction of travel, it became obvious I was going to miss the intended drop zone. With no place to go except down, I found myself heading straight into a freshly fertilized Korean rice patty. It was fertilized with organics from their famous "honey buckets"; think sewage and use your imagination. I tried very hard to land standing, but the wind pulled me backward before I could release myself from the canopy. I found myself lying flat on my back in this pond of cold, nasty stuff, which was slowly seeping in under my helmet. Through no fault of my own, my good day had suddenly become a very bad day.

My buddies came to my rescue, but because of my stench, they wouldn't let me ride in the warm cab of the truck. The weather was very cold, with about a two-hour drive back to our base. Along the way, they decided to stop at an NCO club to have a beer. I was freezing and wet, but I smelled so bad they wouldn't allow me inside to get a drink. I drank a cold beer while sitting on some of our equipment in back of the truck. My double-good day had now become a double-bad day. After what seemed like an eternity, we arrived back at our quanset hut on base. There was more bad news, because then I had to strip and hose off with frigidly cold water before being allowed inside. My body had changed color from light tan to pale white, with light-blue rings around my lips and fingernails. My good day had now become a triple-bad day.

I completed my military service obligation and once again went in search of my road to paradise. My search continued taking shape as I walked further and further away from my loving family circle. Or so I thought. My agenda was simple: I would no longer be encumbered by the outdated principles my parents held so dear, especially those boring, lame words of wisdom that had come from those older folks I knew. They seemed to think they held the patent on knowledge and knew everything about everything, especially about me and how I should live my life. I was free now to write my own rules; go where I wanted, when I wanted, do what I wanted, and above all I wouldn't be held accountable to anyone but myself.

It was a wonderful plan but one built on youthful ignorance; it didn't take long, however, to run head on into reality, where it stalled, crashed, and burned. I found myself confronted by the cold, hard facts of life, sadly realizing my concept of life and the true facts of life weren't even in the same playbook. I discovered that not just my road but also anyone's road to paradise is seldom experienced in tranquil settings but rather through one's harsh encounters with the realities of life itself. I would have to change playbooks. My good days seemed to get lost in the simple question "Is this all life has to offer?" Even though I knew meaning and purpose gave fullness and completion to life, there had to be better days ahead.

My insistent attitude that I would control my own destiny had resulted in total astigmatism. The guiding light of my life had become blurred, and my goals became hidden in confusion. I knew I had chosen the wrong fork in the road and would have to turn around and go back to my original point of reference. This deep-seated truth I could always return to, regardless of my circumstance, was my family circle. My parents had paid the price and painstakingly built a loving and unified family circle. It was centered on biblical teachings, which were taught daily to all of us kids while we were seated around the table. They taught us godly principals as a family unit that not only defined our purpose and meaning in life but also helped to lighten our individual paths along our roads to paradise.

I decided to install a data dump and then proceeded to delete the entire concept of "I will do it my way." I then humbly started from scratch and installed my new and improved concept of "I will do it God's way." His ways have been around forever, but they were new to me despite my parental upbringing. This was a major reversal for me, since I thought I would lose everything I held dear; instead I lost nothing and gained everything, including an eternal home in heaven. The program was built around the following: God's ways weren't mine, His thoughts were higher than mine, and therefore I wouldn't have to bother about relying on my own understanding. My new playbook was titled the "Holy Bible." I was surprised to find that my new playbook totally restructured my priorities in life. It didn't even recognize houses, cars, pride, status, power, fame, or fortune as examples of paradise. Instead, the Holy Spirit revealed paradise to me in terms of two red wine glasses, a lawnmower, and a beautician, along with numerous other things—all people related. I couldn't imagine experiencing paradise in so many wonderful ways. During this process, I stumbled upon an oxymoron. "The price I paid for the car I was driving wasn't for the vehicle but rather for the trip I was planning to take with it."

Spiritually, I finally woke up, drove through that narrow gate, and merged onto a long, narrow, and winding road, my road to paradise. Along the way I encountered so many wonderful people, but I cherish my relationships with Rose, Joseph, and Mona above all the others I met along the way. At different times of my life, each walked with me as I journeyed along the narrow road I was traveling. Through the circumstances of their lives and my relationship with each of them, I had discovered "my road to paradise." Their influence on my life taught me the true meaning of what it means to have good days or bad days. I realized that days aren't defined by happiness or sadness, good or bad, not even by failures or successes. These emotions will ebb and flow, rise and fall continually during our daily walk. Instead, good or bad days are defined by the quality of each day experienced and how it reaches beyond us. In other words, how does each day influence the lives of others we encounter? The joy that comes from a personal relationship with Christ overrides both the good days and bad days so all days are good regardless of the hardships we face. Perhaps some days feel better than others, but I have discovered that regardless of the circumstances we encounter, all days are good when lived out within the joy of the Son of God.

The relationships I have encountered as I traveled along my road to paradise have taught me that value, everlasting value, can be found only in the joy of Jesus Christ; this precious joy underscores every encounter along our journey through life. This relationship quite literally took on the nature of life within itself as I approached what appeared to be the last mile of my earthly journey and final destination. My faith and hope in Christ came face-to-face with the reality of eternity. The Son of God proved His reality to me with one simple act of joy—God is enough.

The table of contents is progressive; it travels from the concept of the family circle, and then engages one in a way of life that leads to life eternal with Jesus Christ.

The Family Circle
Chapter 1

Two hearts—the heart of our heavenly Father and the heart of man—exist independently, but when blended together, they give birth to a new heart. The heart of God infused into the family circle, God's building block for humanity. This is the crown jewel of His creation and stands alone as the most resilient institution ever introduced into the world. The family circle is not hereditary. The parents must first plant the seeds, cultivate the relationships, and provide uninterrupted opportunities for Christ-centered growth. Their principles, examples, and teachings produce the harvest that nourishes the lives of both their children and future generations. Fortunately my road to paradise was rooted in this type of family environment. It was built on godly principles and nurtured by both of my parents. They encouraged and promoted a way of life they knew would lead their family not only through this life on earth but also to an eternal home in heaven, where there would be everlasting joy.

The family circle was conceived in the mind of God given the breath of life by Him, and ultimately birthed through our first ancestors, Adam and Eve. They were created in the image of God and given dominion over all living things on earth. God entrusted the care of all other created life to man, but because the family circle is so precious, He reserved its care for Himself. The beautiful narrative found in Genesis 1–3 tells the story of Adam and Eve along with creation.

As the Father of both of them, God performed the earth's first wedding ceremony uniting Adam and Eve in marriage. It began with only the two of them, and now through them, God's plans for humanity's long, treacherous journey through life began. This embedded and unchangeable precedent has always been nothing more, or nothing less, than the marriage of one man to one woman. From this the family circle would grow to fulfill God's purpose as it traveled through the ages of time. Our heavenly Father's ultimate goal is to choose from these travelers a future bride for His Son (the saved in Christ). Along the way, those chosen as the bride of Christ will be invited to our Father's home in heaven, where they will be seated at the table of the marriage supper of the Lamb. Our heavenly Father's plan finds completion through His Son's marriage to an earthly bride, who then becomes a member of the eternal family circle of God.

Our heavenly Father set in stone the profound importance of the family circle at the beginning of time. Its value to us, however, is experienced every day on a personal level; yet its purpose is fulfilled as it travels from generation to generation. It began with Adam and Eve's unfortunately acquired knowledge of good and evil; this failure sadly resulted in their expulsion from the Garden of Eden. Adam lived 930 years, and his life overlapped the first 243 years of Methuselah. Methuselah lived 969 years, and his life overlapped the first 600 years of Noah. The family circle, illustrated through the lives of these men, traveled from the Garden of Eden 1,656 years through time to Noah and the flood.

Moses wrote in Genesis 4–6 that during this period, with few exceptions, humanity chose evil over good. Wickedness prevailed during this period. It was so intense that it greatly grieved God's heart. With the exception of Noah, his wife, his three sons, and their wives, God's plans of greatness for the family circle had collapsed into chaos, corruption, and violence. He now deeply regretted creating human beings on the earth. But Noah, a just man who walked with God, found grace in the LORD'S sight. Therefore, God told Noah to build an ark, a seafaring vessel, a safe haven for him and his wife, their three sons along with their wives, and all the living creatures he would be instructed to bring on board. Eventually they would repopulate the earth.

God instructed Noah to build an ark 300 cubits (510 feet) long and 50 cubits (85 feet) wide and 30 cubits (51 feet) high. Although Noah was quite overwhelmed, he was obedient to God and did everything he was instructed to do. It was a daunting task, but he commenced immediately with the work set before him. For Noah and his family, it was a long and laborious project, taking somewhere between fifty and seventy-five years to complete. When the work was completed, the LORD instructed Noah to bring his wife and their three sons—Shem, Ham, and Japheth—along with their wives into the ark. Noah also brought all the living creatures God had chosen into the ark. God closed the door of the ark behind them in the six hundredth year, second month, and seventeenth day of his life. On that very day, the floodgates of heaven were opened, and for forty days and nights, torrential, uninterrupted rain commenced. The water covered the earth to more than fifteen cubits (25.5 feet) above the high mountaintops. Every person, animal, and creature living on the face of the earth perished; all were totally destroyed, wiped out. After 150 long days, the waters began to recede, and once again dry land appeared. Noah and his family, along with all the animals and creatures, joyfully proceeded to leave the ark.

In his generation Noah was a righteous man who, in the depraved generation in which he lived, found grace in God's sight. As such, God saved him and his family from total destruction. The first family circle, Adam and Eve, was relegated to life on earth outside the garden because of their disobedience to God; now the LORD would breathe new life into the family circle through Noah's family because of their obedience to Him. Noah's obedience and subsequent salvation from destruction by the flood are perfect bookends of our heavenly Father's ongoing expectations for parents today.

The greatest burden and most important responsibility placed on the shoulders of parents is the governance of their own family circle. It starts with obedience to our heavenly Father and a relationship with His Son. It progresses to marriage and little babies, who become the receptors of their parents' godly wisdom and subsequently the building blocks for the generations that follow. Parents along with the children who follow become the reference point that serves to steer the family circle through every encounter life offers them.

The family circle in so many ways resembles the weaver's loom. It contemplates the analogy of a spindle that goes back and forth countless times as it weaves its way to completion; all the while, the unfinished work lies hidden in decisions yet to be made. These decisions are represented by an array of colored threads resting on a nearby table offering a palette of life choices. These choices eventually emerge into the image of a living organism, the family circle. With each pass the spindle renders an image of decisions past, along with a partial picture of life to come. Finally, as the last mile approaches completion, the parents stand back and observe their labor, the product of a life filled with choices and its finished work. A finished work that illustrates the key that one day will unlock the gate to eternity.

Although the original model began in ancient times, my journey began in a period normally referred to as "modern times." But despite the many generational, religious, cultural, and ceremonial changes, God's rules for the modern family circle haven't changed from old. They are forever tethered to the truth embedded in its ancient origin. The family circle is without credibility if the sinew that binds it to its original heritage is altered or severed. God had no intentions of allowing His original plan to be reshaped to accommodate deviant lifestyles, which would lead to the modern-day mutation of the family circle. On the contrary, modern society is greatly blessed with resources that afford it numerous opportunities to comprehend and participate in God's plan for marriage, thus achieving His ultimate purpose for the family circle.

God's plan of marriage and subsequent family is much more than a pro-life plan. It also sets the moral standard for our relationships with others. He established the family circle within the sanctity of marriage and celibacy outside of marriage. The marriage structure resembles the nature of a commonwealth, one that draws its resources from God, its core; then it extends that influence through the parents to all its members. God gave this principle; its worth is found in God, and His purpose is satisfied through a marital relationship between man and woman. The central characters and hierarchy of the family circle are the Father, Son, Holy Spirit, and parents; it's an unchangeable and everlasting chain of command. It is totally unique in that it is a global concept that crosses the boundaries of all nations, religions, cultures, and traditions while keeping the ancient example intact. Even so, it demands navigation through Christ-centered parents, for without them the family will drift aimlessly with no sense of value or direction.

According to the 2010 US Census Bureau, there are about 117,379,845 households in the United States, with approximately 2.58 persons per family. The fabric, character, and behavior of each of these are vastly different; even though commonalities remain ingrained, they all mature with different belief systems and purposes. This is true, but God in His infinite wisdom provided the world with a universal moral standard, which supersedes religion, culture, or tradition. His guiding principles are written in the Bible, where the reader is introduced to the holy Trinity—the Father, Son, and Holy Spirit. Through their leading, He defines marriage, from which the family circle emerges; next comes the role of parents, along with countless other commands and instructions designed for righteous daily living. Construction of a healthy family circle is a continuing process that takes on many shapes, but the fabric that binds it together is always the same. Our loving Father put it this way: "Start children off on the way they should go, and even when they are old they will not turn from it." (Proverbs (22:6). "Father, do not exasperate your children; instead, bring them up in the training and instruction of the Lord" (Ephesians 6:4).

The most important contribution parents can make to their family is found in the last statement: Parents, "train and instruct your children in the ways of the Lord." That was a universal statement directed to a global audience. No child should ever be deprived of this teaching or of a parent's love; this is a constant reference point for parents so they may prepare their children for their long and arduous journeys through life. This principle demands parental investment not only in time, resources, and instruction but also in example as the family engages in the daily rigors of life. His instructions are explicit and must be arrested by the parents—taken into custody, accepted, and conformed to. Parents then must teach this Christ-centered lifestyle to their children and their children's children. These commands aren't simply suggestions but imperatives. Noah and the flood are a great example of choices and ensuing consequences.

Our loving Father planted the seed for the family circle a long time ago and not without purpose. Regardless of your perspective as a corporate body (church), family circle, or individual, the journey and end result are the same. The journey is a time filled with individual preparation for one's eternal future. Beginning with Adam and Eve, the first family, God has satisfied man's desire for a relationship with each other through marriage. Now through Christ, our Savior, He then satisfies His own desire for a relationship with us. From the life our heavenly Father had created, His Son would now choose a bride for Himself. Through His Son and His chosen bride, the Father would forever establish and solidify His eternal relationship with humanity. Upon completion of their earthly journey, the bride of Christ will enter through heaven's gate as an invited guest to the marriage supper of the Lamb, where it will be welcomed as our heavenly Father's family circle, and the eternal family of God. The Father's plan became a reality when His Son came to earth to choose His bride.

God didn't offer a dowry; instead, He paid a "bride's price," which came in the form of a proposal. The proposal was addressed to humanity; it declared, "I love you so much that I am offering you the privilege of becoming the bride of Christ, my child. 'I ask of you only one thing: Do you believe that He, Jesus, is my Son, the Son of God? If you accept my proposal and believe in Him, then I will make reservations for you at the marriage supper of the Lamb.'" But the proposal was so much more than an offer to the offspring of Adam and Eve. It was God's 783,137-word proposal to His Son's future bride. It is often referred to as "God's love letter" to mankind, the Bible. Rightfully so, since He sacrificed His only Son's life to prove His love for us—an example of the type of love parents should live out within their own family circle.

The chosen bride, which being those of us who have citizenship in the Father's earthly kingdom, have now been adopted into the Father's eternal family circle. God chose the earthly family circle as the instrument through which He would propagate the earth and accomplish His ultimate purpose. Now, as the bride of Christ, He will populate the holy hills of heaven through His Son. Amazing! It's the Father's desire that every member of the family—including mom, dad, and children, along with all others under their guardianship—complete the journey without one member being lost. His ultimate goal is for an unbroken family circle, where every member is present at the marriage supper of the Lamb, the most beautiful wedding ceremony ever imagined.

The old hymn "Will the Circle Be Unbroken" is one of my favorite gospel songs. The song title speaks of our loving Father's desire for all families. It should have special appeal to every parent, since it looks ahead to a time and place where the family circle once again becomes united and complete; all are seated around the table of the marriage supper of the Lamb. It also speaks to a broken family circle, a dysfunctional family that could possibly have been mended with nothing more than a small drop of love and forgiveness.

We often associate and limit our knowledge of God to the daily encounters we experience in our lives. With this assumption, suppose I ask you to choose a geometric shape you come in contact with on a daily basis, one that can be used to fully represent the Bible, the Father, the Son, the Holy Spirit, and earthly parents; it's one that also encompasses the physical, spiritual, and eternal aspects of the family circle. What would you choose? I have sifted through each of the different geometric shapes and arrived at one obvious conclusion: The circle. It is the only shape known to mankind that has an absolute spiritual, mathematical, and physical center point that remains fixed regardless of size and orientation. It occupies a common place in almost every aspect of our lives. It is indicative of the Father as the center of creation, the Son as the center of God's love for humanity, the Holy Spirit as the center of the relationship between the Father and Son, the Bible as the center of God's written instruction to humanity, and parents as the center of God's will for the completeness of the family circle. It is multifaceted since it represents the language of God's love along with the disciplines of science and mathematics. The unit circle is also home to the most popular of all mathematical constants, and it is all about that tiny but necessary dot located in the absolute center and what it can represent.

Regardless of time and distance, we can never travel beyond the parameters of God's love. It flows from our loving Father, where love originates through His Son, the instrument of God's love; through the Holy Spirit, the voice of His love; through parents, the object of His love; and then finally into the family circle, the beneficiary of His love. Together these are life's reference or default points. They have everlasting consequences, but as with all human endeavors, they must begin with the first step. We must start by building our own personal road to paradise, where the pure and perfect objective is to arrive with an unbroken family circle at the gates of heaven.

There is no sacrifice too great or effort too small that shouldn't be invested whenever possible into the family circle. The greatest privilege ever given to a parent is to teach and establish his or her children in the ways of the Lord. Of all life's endeavors, it is the most important, since it is the cornerstone of God's plan for humanity, His primary building block. As the family threads are selected and woven together, the tapestry must ultimately evolve into the image of a road that leads to an eternal home in heaven with Christ. It must culminate in a journey in search of paradise, a road that depicts mountains climbed and valleys left behind. This tapestry must represent a road that fades into the last mile of a long journey, one that ends with knowledge of the best yet to come.

God performed the first wedding ceremony, which gave birth to the first family circle, but He didn't walk away and leave its fruit to ripen and then fall to the ground. Our heavenly Father brought life into this world for a purpose that engages the vitality of life from within the family circle and a wholesome home environment. It develops from within the center of the circle, the parents, using our heavenly Father's playbook. It is the perfect guide, play by play, to guide the family circle to an everlasting home in heaven. But unless parents allow God to build the house and Christ to make it into a home, it won't stand against the gate of eternity.

The Table

Chapter 2

I have read numerous articles titled "What Makes a House a Home?" After reading several, I was disappointed, although not surprised that most of them centered on location, brick and mortar, and creature comforts. Of all the articles I read, not one of them fully addressed the true meaning of what makes a house a home. It is a complex question, especially when you attempt to reduce these three points to the lowest common denominator. But then after weeks or even months of riding an emotional roller coaster, you are finally forced to admit there is no simple answer to making this often or once-in-a-lifetime major investment. Then you join the masses, take the leap, and buy a house, all with one thought in mind: I hope I am making the right choice.

Why is this? According to the US Census Bureau, there were 1,228,000 new residential housing starts in October 2018; each of them was just another house situated on a plot of ground. I don't believe it's the house that makes a home but the family circle living in it; that family transforms the house into a home. The house is a reflection of hopefully good choices, but the family is the embodiment of life in a home. It is a place where every member has a sense of belonging to something that is special, totally his or hers; it's a place where memories are built that no one can ever erase.

Every home is authentic in its own right; each has its own personality, which in large part is developed around the creature comforts for the family. Excluding location and brick and mortar, I asked several people what single item contributed most to making their house into a home. Their answers were all over the map, and once again I was disappointed because I didn't get the answer I wanted to hear. They responded with favorite items, such as their bed, pet, books, recliner, entertainment room furnishings, TV, china cabinet, makeup mirror, computer, and so forth. Granted, all these certainly fill either a functional or indulgent purpose in the home, but none included the answer I was hoping to hear. Most of the responses centered on creature comforts or assets with monetary value. Also, most of the responses centered on self (for example, my recliner, my bed, and so forth). I hoped to hear an answer that identified something mutually beneficial to the entire family. I was looking for that one item that would promote personal growth, encourage communication, mold bonds, build loving relationships, and open doors of opportunity. Something special that not only contributed to making the house a home but also enriched the lives of everyone in the home far beyond its monetary worth.

I chose the breakfast or dining room table, which is nothing more than a piece of furniture with a flat top and usually supported by four or more legs. It could be ornate or plain, wooden or glass. I chose it because, if removed from the kitchen or dining room, it would leave a space no other piece of furniture could fill; its absence would create a vacuum that would deprive the family of so many treasured moments. Like the circle, when its analogy as the center point of the family circle is considered, its value quickly rises above all other items in the home. It is the perfect platform from which to launch the wisdom inherent within the family circle. The environment created around it is unique above all other furnishings, mainly because of its special ability as a common meeting place, serving to bring the family together. Many comforts of home are realized in other furnishings, but the atmosphere surrounding the table is the magic wand that transforms a house into a home where families come together. It begins at the tabletop, where the parents' sphere of influence is spread throughout the home, where every item bears their signature—their mark of love and compassion.

The table serves as an ideal platform, from where the family is nurtured and grows into maturity. It engages every aspect of the family circle by serving as a focal point for teaching, learning, relationships, special occasions, and family discussions about things that matter. Things like Christian values, Thanksgiving, Christmas, Easter, and other special days, all of which serve as building blocks that grow the family into God's intended purpose. Opportunities like enlightening Dad to the fact that perhaps his little girls also enjoy hunting and fishing; or that playing the piano may also be of interest to his little boys. The table is an ideal starting point, from where family dynamics begin to take shape. Family members interacting around the table portray the image of love, sharing, bonding, and mending along with a world of other unforgettable memories. It's also the birthplace of a lifetime of guidance and resources. It's where the family circle receives its life and purpose.

I say this because no matter how much time, expense, and effort go into making a house into a home, it is never complete without the ultimate goal of an eternal home in heaven together. Completion is found in a home where Christ is the centerpiece of the family. The true meaning of this eternal hope is found in the words "I'm going home." These are beautiful words, reaching far beyond our earthly home and looking forward into the reality of a coming eternal resting place, a final destination and heavenly home. Hope, this is another one of those rare words that through faith looks forward to Christ and eventually will end in the truth of His reality.

But let's not underestimate the table's value as a convenient elbow prop, especially when exasperation seems to rule the day. There are many times when Mom and Dad looked across the table in amazement, marveling at how they survived the day. They probably looked at us kids and prayed we would grow into adults before we killed each other in some crazy scheme that no one, not even ourselves, could understand. Then, lo and behold, their dreams began to come true; the kids grow into young adults (fifteen or sixteen years of age), as evidenced by junior coming home with a classic statement. "Dad, I wrecked the car, but it wasn't my fault." Patience is indeed a virtue.

Sundays were always special for our family. Everyone without exception was seated around the table for Sunday dinner. Times were good. Dad was employed by International Paper Company, enjoyed a good income, and provided well for his family. Then suddenly, without warning, everything changed. At the age of thirty-eight, he suffered a massive heart attack that left him totally disabled; our main source of income abruptly ended, and the family income dropped to fifty-two dollars per month. For a family of six, this meager amount presented the image of a mountain too steep to climb. The loss of Dad's health and income introduced the beginning of many sacrifices for our family. I was twelve years old at the time, the oldest boy of four siblings, and there were two more babies on the horizon. It seemed that my whole world had suddenly turned upside down. My dreams of paradise that had gathered around shiny new cars, pretty girls, lots of money, fame and fortune—all faded into the reality of becoming a twelve-year-old family breadwinner. The small farm that had once been a hobby now became our family's primary means of survival.

As a twelve-year-old farm boy, life suddenly became very confusing and difficult; during school months, my typical day started at about four a.m. and ended around ten thirty at night. There were farm chores from four to six a.m., a thirty-seven-mile one-way bus ride to school, and a return home for more chores and/or plowing fields until sometimes late at night. Doing homework and studying assignments were done on the school bus or not at all. In the mid-1950s, electricity hadn't yet reached our rural community. Today's necessities, had they been available to us, would have been considered luxuries. Cutting firewood for heating and cooking was a daily necessity. Then there were all the animals to feed and water, along with our family's requirements of water for cooking and bathing. Since we didn't have running water in the house, drawing water from the well was a daily never-ending challenge. And lest I forget, there were cows to milk; then I was back to farming duties, which included tending a large vegetable garden.

Our main crops were corn and cotton. We planted and cultivated the crops with a two-row International tractor. I was a scrawny kid but luckily strong enough to drive our tractor, even though it offered quite a challenge. It should have been above my physical ability, but I soon realized that necessity is the father of "where there is a will there is a way." After all, it was my job, born out of necessity, and not optional. I would grasp the bottom of the steering wheel with one hand, slipped down out of the seat, pressed the clutch, shifted gears with the other hand, and quickly jumped back onto the seat; it was a typical routine—row after row after row. Because of my limitations, my rows weren't always perfectly straight. This fact irritated my dad; he expected symmetry and perfectly straight rows. His occasional dissatisfaction with me was discouraging, but I knew my physical capacity, and I accepted it, knowing it wasn't going to change until I grew bigger and stronger. I was already giving it my best effort; I had no more to give. As time went by, I realized criticism wasn't his objective. He was teaching me in his own loving way that there is always room for improvement—a principle I've learned to practice throughout my life.

Reflecting back on those days, I see that my future looked pretty dim at times, but from somewhere deep inside, my desire to succeed proved sufficient to keep the light of hope burning within me. Mom was my inspiration; my allowance was her smile of approval, which said, "I love you, Son." She seemed to know I understood that through God's provision everything would be okay.

Our world didn't hold a place, in my opinion, more inviting than the dining table on Thanksgiving Day. It was in every sense a special day that added a special ingredient into transforming a house into a home. The Pilgrims first celebrated Thanksgiving in October 1621, and the day has been celebrated as a federal holiday since 1863, when President Lincoln proclaimed the last Thursday of November as the official day of celebration. My dad gave life to Thanksgiving by celebrating God as the center of our family. He accepted God as the center of his life, and then by his example and teachings, God became the center of our lives as well. Dad first offered thanksgiving to his loving Father for choosing him as His servant, for watching over Mom and us kids. He thanked God for the bountiful blessing of a smokehouse filled with hams, slabs of bacon, and other salted meats; for a barn filled with corn and hay; and for money from the sale of the harvest. A good harvest meant there would probably be a nice surprise from Santa Claus come Christmas, so in every respect the blessings justified the celebration.

As expected, Mom and my sister lovingly prepared the most engaging event of the day and laid it out on the table of Thanksgiving. It was a much-anticipated occasion; we were at home, where we would always find a chair for our comfort and a plate filled with love. Beside the plate, there was a glass of joy along with a knife to gently cut away the pressures of life. The setting also included a spoonful of happiness, and then there were two forks that completed the table setting. The first fork was used for eating from the table's gracious bounty. Then after everyone finished eating, the table was cleared, and the leftover food, along with all the utensils except the second fork, was returned to the kitchen. It was reserved for something special. That second fork symbolized that the best was yet to come, a dessert Mom had baked in the oven of a wood-burning stove. It was the last course of a wonderful meal and always an opportunity for everyone to chime in and talk about lots of things that mattered. There were also empty chairs standing along the wall in memory of those whom the Father had already called home to sit at His heavenly table. Then, to complete the table arrangement, a beautiful white linen napkin was placed beside every plate.

The popular TV series *The Waltons* portrayed a fictional family, whose lives in many ways resembled my upbringing. It seems that in every episode the viewing audience watched this fictional family gather around the dining or kitchen table. Before each meal, a loving father, Papa Walton, always offered a prayer of thanksgiving for the many blessings bestowed on his family. From their vantage points, the parents would discuss the important issues of the day with each other, the grandparents, and the children. By the end of the meal, the entire family walked away in lockstep with a good understanding of what was expected from each of them. The parents were in all circumstances the personification of love, family, and community. Our family seated around the table, especially on Thanksgiving Day, lived out the fictional Walton family drama. It was special, like the soft texture of a warm blanket draped over one's shoulders on a cold day; it brought total contentment.

Christmas around the world was and still is the most significant of all days, not just holidays. In AD 336 the Emperor of Rome, Constantine, declared Christianity a legal religion. A few years later, the church officially designated December 25 as the birth date of Jesus Christ. In 1836 Alabama became the first state to recognize Christmas as an official state holiday. Then, on December 25, 1870, President Grant declared Christmas an official federal holiday. Dad and Mom celebrated Christmas like no other day of the year; they were living, breathing, and walking testimonies of their love for Christ. They accepted Him as the Redeemer, Savior, and centerpiece of their family and home. They understood God's love for all humanity. Our parents' cause for celebration was much different from ours. Their joy was twofold: They celebrated the birth of Christ along with the joy that comes from giving. As kids it was one dimensional; we saw it as a night when Santa passed by to leave special gifts for each of us, so come Christmas morning, both our parents and we kids received equal gratification. Joy was twice received—our parents through giving, we children from receiving. And finally, there was always the joy of having Christ in our home.

Christmas was always awesome, and naturally we kids were focused on Santa Claus. That day was the most important of all days; everything else in the whole world could wait. I especially remember my twelfth Christmas morning. We got up early to check under the tree to make sure Santa had stopped to deliver our much-anticipated and deserved presents. As expected, he had indeed stopped and left gifts for each of us. Although the wrapping paper was different, my younger brother noticed that his present and mine were in identically sized boxes. This caused a low level of concern since each of us wanted something uniquely different from the other. But the momentary distress turned to excitement when we opened the boxes and saw what was inside—unimaginable and huge. My younger brother and I were each given a shiny, new Daisy BB gun. They were pump air rifles that were so powerful we were convinced we could now start hunting big game. We could go on safari to hunt for lions and bull elephants in the jungles around our farm; we even protected new settlers from wild Indians and captured notorious bank robbers with the loot they had stolen. We would become young legends in our own time.

Endless opportunities lay ahead, so we immediately began planning hunting expeditions along with other exciting things. Then Dad got involved and came up with all these rules about what we could and couldn't do with our guns. So, of course, we quickly developed our own set of rules. After all, we were so smart. We could now hunt and shoot big game when our parents weren't around, and in short it was open season for anything, providing of course that we didn't get caught. Living on a farm offered bountiful opportunities, but for the most part, we restricted our hunting activities to chasing down bank robbers and wild Indians. Occasionally we went on safari to hunt for big game, especially ferocious chickens; our chicken yard was full of them. On these expeditions we hunted, stalked, and then shot our prey from a safe distance. We waited until one of these predators came into range, and being incredible marksmen, we scored with every shot. Actually, we were never in real danger since they lived in a large fenced-in yard. We only pumped our BB guns twice so the velocity wouldn't kill or injure the chicken. We didn't know it at the time, but later, following a serious confrontation with Dad, we discovered that chickens were a protected species on our farm.

Picture this: It was Sunday, our special family day and a few weeks after Christmas. We all got up early, dressed in our Sunday best, and then after passing mom's inspection, we went to church. We attended Sunday school, followed by the worship service; and then we kids stood around outside while our parents carried on lots of small talk with the other church folks. Finally, we went home to eat Sunday dinner. We were having free-range southern-fried chicken, straight from the chicken yard, through Mom's magical kitchen and then onto our dinner table. There were also home-grown organic vegetables, mashed potatoes, and hand-made baked biscuits; and lest I forget, there was always dessert. This completed our Sunday dinner. Mom's culinary skills were the best; her attention to detail in our home and especially the scrumptious meals she placed on the table were some of the primary ingredients that went into making our house a home.

Dad took his customary place at the head of the table. He said grace, giving thanks to Jesus Christ for all the blessings we had received. He was a big man; he was six foot and one inch tall, and he weighed about 240 pounds. He carried himself well. He smiled often but still spoke with lots of authority. I can honestly say I never heard him curse or even raise his voice in anger. His easy-going manner and quick smile were his signature character traits. His smile revealed a white porcelain cap on one of his upper front teeth. A narrow gold band surrounded the outer edges of the white porcelain. Following our usual protocol, Dad served himself and then passed the plate around the table, where we, in turn, served ourselves. Mom always waited until last, ensuring everyone else had first been served with plenty. But we loved and appreciated Mom so much that we made sure her favorites always remained on the platter. I'm old school and still subscribe to the adage that "the hand that rocks the cradle rules the world;" and if it didn't rock the cradle, it certainly ruled our home.

Dad took a big bite from his drumstick, and suddenly his expression changed. I noticed that he was moving the chicken around in his mouth as if searching for something. By now, my heart had dropped to my knees, since I knew something no one else other than my younger brother knew. The suspense ended when he gently pushed something with his tongue, and it dropped from between his lips into the palm of his hand. He very deliberately placed it on the table in front of his plate for everyone to see. It was a broken, shiny, white porcelain tooth cap. My heart literally jumped for joy because I had expected to see something other than a tooth cap. My brother and I exchanged grateful glances, but our euphoria was short lived. Dad's tongue continued to search. Then he found it; with his thumb and pointing finger, he took from between his lips a small, round three-sixteenths-diameter shiny ball. But this time, my heart didn't stop at my knees; it went straight to the floor in search of a place of refuge, anywhere other than where I was. I needed a place to hide; we were busted. It was a BB, the result of one of our many hunting expeditions.

Yep! You guessed it. This particular Sunday, our special day, wasn't going to have a good ending. It wasn't a good day! I could feel it in my bones; I just knew this was going to be a life-changing event. With his usual calm demeanor, he looked at me and said, "Son, when you finish eating your dinner, I want to see you in your bedroom." My usual place of rest had suddenly erupted into my worst nightmare.

Yes, my younger brother was also invited to participate. We were severely disciplined, although I wouldn't call it a beating; Dad wasn't that kind of person. The pain inflicted by the belt would soon go away, but what bothered us most was what he said afterwards. He didn't ask how many chickens we had shot but simply said, "If I ever find another BB in one of the chickens, I am going to whip you both again, and it's going to be one you will never forget." I was taught many valuable lessons while growing up, but this experience taught me how to grade, kill, remove the feathers, inspect, and re-inspect chickens before they went to Mom's kitchen in preparation for our meals. I didn't know how many chickens we had shot, but what I did know was that fried chicken for Sunday dinner would never be the same again. The possibility remained that I had overlooked that one little spot. *Webster's* didn't have to explain the definition of *consequence* to me, because from that moment on, the meaning was forever engraved in my mind. I've since discovered, depending on the source and environment, that the life expectancy of a farm chicken ranges from five to ten years and in rare cases up to sixteen years. That's a long time to worry about something as small as a BB.

Perhaps I was too young and immature to appreciate the tabletop education I received while growing up. I think my parents did understand this, but they never allowed my response to their teachings and guidance to alter their core beliefs. Dad was a minister, and like any other parent, he wanted all his children to grow up and make him proud. His goal was to clothe each of us in a robe of righteousness, which comes solely from a personal relationship with Christ. Dad and Mom embraced and arrested God's moral standards, and they accepted custodial responsibility. While seated around the table, they locked these standards into us kids' hearts so tightly that they could never escape.

As a minister, Dad also understood that his journey to paradise was built on faith and hope in Christ. He knew his last mile and final destination would come to rest in heaven. As a child, I didn't yet have that insight. But what I did understand and appreciate was the value of a loving family, honesty, work ethics, responsibility, accountability, and above all a foundation rooted in godly principles. These enabled me to venture out into a world of unknowns, a world filled with opportunities for both success and failure. These values taught me to be my own person, confident in my decisions and always willing to accept responsibility along with the consequences of my actions.

I completed a seventeen-year conversation with my parents on the virtues of life, my tabletop education, along with lots of hands-on work and play experience mixed in. This period would now slowly fade into the sunset, although I would cherish and carry its memories with me throughout my life. My parents and siblings were the image of an ideal family circle.

Because of Dad's illness, I became accustomed to making many decisions at a young age. As a result, leading up to my graduation, I became a very independent-minded person, and although Dad's guiding principles had never failed me, they were nevertheless too restrictive for the lifestyle I envisioned for myself. I arrived at one simple conclusion—change my wardrobe. Although I would always remember my reference point—the family circle and my tabletop education—I replaced the robe of Christ Dad had tried to wrap around me with my own choices. I wasn't ready to don a robe of righteousness. Rather than being clothed in Christ, I designed my own wardrobe to wear in search of my road to paradise.

The Road

Chapter 3

My concept of a road to paradise began to materialize as a junior in high school. Up to that point, it had been only a dream, but now, watching my childhood dreams slowly develop into reality, it was becoming more and more exciting. The highlights of the journey itself would cancel out all the disappointments I expected to encounter along the way. One of the most unforgettable was my junior/senior prom. As the date for this all-important event approached, I conjured up visions of myself dressed in a black tuxedo and escorting the most beautiful young lady in the whole world. The problem was that I had no money, no transportation, and no prospects in sight.

I developed a plan: I went to my sister who was a senior and asked whether I could double-date with her and her boyfriend. She discussed the idea with him, and they reluctantly agreed, but only if I for certain had a date. The most beautiful girl in the world just happened to be the head majorette at a nearby high school in our neighboring county. Since we did have a casual acquaintance, as the saying goes, I had nothing to lose by asking. Although I was very apprehensive because I was afraid, on one hand, she would say yes, while at the same time I would be devastated if she were to say no.

Finally, I mustered up enough courage to pop the big question, and much to my surprise, she said yes. Now I really had a dilemma; I still had no money, and it was not only customary but expected of the guy to buy his date a corsage and then take her to a nice restaurant for dinner following this festive occasion. I am not sure how many different ways I came up with to earn the money, but somehow, before the big night arrived, I managed to scrimp and save up about six dollars. My sister and her boyfriend had agreed with me to bring us to an inexpensive restaurant. The prom was beautiful, and I did everything possible to impress my lovely date. She received lots of attention, and I even overheard several of the guys say, "Wow, how did he get a date with her? She is beautiful!" There's an old saying: "Shoot for the moon, and if you miss, you might still hit a star."

Following the prom, we went to a small diner as planned. The waitress gave us a menu, which I quickly scanned, and much to my disappointment, there were only a few items listed that were within my budget of six dollars. My date looked at the menu, then looked at me, and asked, "What are you going to get?" My anxiety meter had long since reached critical mass; I knew when I glanced at the menu choices that I was in trouble. I didn't have enough money to pay for most of the single meals and certainly not enough for two. The waitress was waiting, so I asked my date to order first, and then told her I hadn't yet decided. I couldn't believe the position I had placed myself in; if she ordered something that cost too much, I would be forced to do the unimaginable. A six-dollar excuse would have been small payment in exchange for my crushed pride.

My heart had long since stopped beating; it was taking forever for her to make up her beautiful mind, but she finally looked up at the waitress, smiled, and said, "I will have the fried catfish with french fries." My heart rate jumped from zero to at least 150 beats per minute. Her prom dinner was going to cost me about $5.50 including tax and drink. My arithmetic told me I had fifty cents left. I was so hungry, but I smiled at the waitress and told her I had a stomachache but would like something sweet anyway, so I ordered a Hershey's chocolate bar. We all enjoyed our meal, and afterward we left the diner, and I drove her home. While walking her to the front door, she told me that she really had a wonderful evening, and then before going inside, she put her arms around me and gave me a really sweet goodnight kiss. She was my first date and first kiss; total success, a really good day. I love it when well-thought-out plans come together.

A few months later, while serving in the army in Korea, I received a Dear John letter from her. While reading her letter, it became obvious to me that her ambitions had grown far beyond my reach, especially at that time. It wasn't a good day, but the circumstances surrounding this short-lived romance taught me a guiding principle that has followed me throughout life. Failure is only a stepping-stone to success, which can happen only through attempted successes. I was very likely the poorest kid in my class. I had absolutely nothing to work with outside my own initiative and self-determination; but with a little luck, I dreamed, planned, and executed that night with perfection. After reading her letter, I realized that even a perfect start doesn't always guarantee a perfect ending. I discovered that success doesn't always breed success; rather, in many instances it can be nothing more than a prelude for future failure. But I realized I hadn't failed; I was simply the beneficiary of a well-developed plan that didn't end in a lasting relationship. But from this experience, I discovered many doors of opportunity I hadn't even dreamed of just waiting to be opened. Dreams of my road to paradise slowly materialized as I continued to knock on those doors of opportunity.

As soon as I graduated from high school, I left home, determined to build my own road through life. I was plenty smart; after all, I was seventeen years old. I was going to lay the foundation and then for the first time pave it with my own terms and conditions. I didn't delete, although I did pause my tabletop education along with all those other biblical standards I had been taught. They kept hindering and interfering with my personal plans. I proceeded to upload life links that would connect and integrate me into the way I wanted my life to be lived. I would walk away from the concept of the family circle and tabletop education, which I had received while growing up. I knew my parents wouldn't approve, but I was driven by an anxious mind, sticky eyes, and nervous fingers. I wanted to see, touch, and experience all the previously off-limits things the world had to offer. I envisioned doing things my way—what I wanted, when I wanted, where I wanted, how I wanted, and with whom I wanted. Like I said earlier, I was independently minded and concluded that many of the things I had been taught while seated around the family table were old fashioned and didn't fit well in the fast-paced and contemporary world I now found myself living in.

First, I was willing to sacrifice the comfort and security of my home to escape the rigors of life on the farm. I would walk away from my old life, leaving my family to bear the emotional and physical burden of my decision. Second, the idea of middle- to older-aged folks telling me what, when, where, why, and how I should live my life no longer appealed to me; those outdated demands would soon be abandoned. Those older folks were obviously disconnected from present-day reality, at least as seen through my eyes; after all, I was the product of a new generation. I left the farm behind to go and peel my own onion regardless of the difficulties it imposed on me or others. I was determined to peel it one layer at a time as I searched for my road to paradise. This decision wasn't influenced by an end point but rather by the thrill and excitement experienced along the way.

The sights and sounds of my newfound freedom intrigued me; they were exciting, entertaining, and filled with mystery and discovery. In many ways I envisioned the entertainment and excitement as really good steering mechanisms for my new way of life. I had heard the famous statement "I have a dream" many times, and true, we all have dreams—it's the star we shoot for but seldom hit. I dreamed of a journey along my road to paradise, where I would be a hero much like my uncles, who had come home from World War II. I would have lots of money, because while growing up, I'd had none. I would have a wardrobe filled with lots of nice clothes, since while growing up, I had worn mostly hand-me-downs. I would live in a big, beautiful house, for I had been brought up in an old three-room schoolhouse, which had been remodeled into our home. Above all I would drive a bright, shiny, new car. With my dreams to guide me, I went in search of easy street, the road that would lead me from rags to riches and ultimately fulfill all my dreams. Umm, not so fast; my dreams, I would later discover, had somehow gotten severely disconnected from reality.

"The Road Not Taken," written by Robert Frost in 1916, alerted me to the fact that I had chosen the wrong road. In this classic he represents two roads diverging into a yellow wood. His opening line is a remarkable epiphany that looks into the reality of life through the eyes of three choices: the road less taken, the other road, or a place in the woods. He gives no hint as to what one might encounter along either road; nor does he speculate on the outcome of remaining where he was planted—in the woods. Neither does he allude to the correctness of one choice above the others. But with abundant clarity, he states an imperative: All people must choose the road of life they wish to travel and then accept the consequences of their choice. The imagery found in this classic offered a perfect solution to the road I was searching for. To me it demanded choices that led to unknowns— portals I imagined that framed hidden yet exciting new ways of life. After reading this poem, I became so excited that I was finally getting a chance to embrace these new concepts. Intrigue, mystery, and discovery characterized the poem while, at the same time, clarifying the necessity of decisions.

Perhaps it was from youthful ignorance, but I chose to travel "the other road" represented in the poem because it led me away from the family farm and the tabletop values I had so painstakingly been taught. Although my conscience wasn't entirely happy with my decision, I was nevertheless excited about exploring new horizons. The opportunity held a special appeal for me since it didn't define morality, distinguish good from evil, or even address a final destination. In short, the poem embraced the idea of life as an open door, which allowed me to define and pursue my own goals in life. It epitomized what I thought was my road to paradise. I was excited by his characterization of life, which had been reduced to your choice, your life. Simply stated, my life would now become the aftermath of my own decisions; excitement without responsibility was my first prerequisite. This was indicative of life in its simplest form; roll the dice and live with the consequences.

So I headed down "the other road." After all, my newfound independence gave me the power and privilege to make choices not subject to anyone's or anything's approval but my own. I could finally do it my way since there would be no outside accountability for the choices I made, an approach that was new and exciting to me. In essence, I could travel a road void of responsibility and still achieve my desire of self-satisfaction. What a rush! This no-holds-barred, culture-driven world—a world not encumbered by unknowns that lay on the other side of the forest—allowed me to live life according to my own standards. Since these obscure destinations lived outside the borders of right or wrong, I was no longer concerned with what lay over the next hill or just around the curve in the road. Wow, I thought I was free at last.

I hadn't chosen the road less traveled, because "less traveled" implied restrictions, discipline, and in general rules that didn't support my idea of independence from outside influence. It was reminiscent of another life, the one I had placed on pause. Neither did I choose to remain in the woods simply because I had places to go and things to do and see.

I followed my illusive dreams of paradise for many years before realizing the joy that came from a sense of happiness and well-being had evaporated. I discovered life void of accountability and a sense of direction was also void of love and self-worth. My solution to life and the facts of life did not balance; alas, I had chosen the wrong road. My rocky road was filled with no-win circumstances, a maelstrom of turbulent activity crisscrossed with paths of deception, pleasure void of satisfaction, and elusive dreams of prosperity. My dreams of wealth had melted into the simple fact that money can be obtained only by giving back something of equal or greater value. My road was built from a cacophony of poor choices, which imposed harsh conditions on this traveler. I thought this road would offer guaranteed remedies for all life's ills; but instead of a cure-all, it dead-ended onto numerous lonely roads, sometimes leaving me without resources for a return trip. I had sadly wasted much time that could never be recovered. I found myself in a mental quagmire and unable to make decisions that would lead to lasting value. My sense of direction might best be understood as "trying to find what I was trying to find, with no knowledge of what I was actually looking for." I now found myself as the beneficiary of my own youthful ignorance and bad choices.

My soul was miserable and incomplete. From my past tabletop education, I knew there was a road somewhere on life's horizon that defined the way that ultimately would lead me to the life I was searching for. Eventually, I came to what should have been an obvious conclusion. The options offered in the poem would never lead me to the conclusion of my search, although it did alert me to a simple fact; I had chosen the wrong road. I realized I had been making decisions with only my head and not my heart. At the expense of reality, I had been searching for all the wrong things in all the wrong places. I had slowly but deliberately strayed from my family-taught tabletop values. I found myself being seduced by a world scarred with potholes, broken bridges, and damaged relationships.

I revisited the poem and was amazed to discover a fourth gem of knowledge hidden between its lines. Once again, my dreams, plans, and executions had failed and ended in disappointment. Now I would go in search of a road that would mend the fractures I had ignorantly imposed onto my family circle. There were times when I had sorely stretched the sinews that bound us together, but the circle had never been broken, nor the ties of our family relationships severed. I realized I needed to return to my reference point, the family circle and my tabletop education. From there I could choose a road clearly marked, one with a final destination that offered eternal contentment in lieu of the temporary pleasures of this world. This road would be constructed on a firm foundation, one that could sustain life's heaviest loads. My road would be surfaced to withstand the test of time with bridges that would span the darkest valleys and navigate my life's most turbulent waters.

From the vantage point of my childhood days, the little light in my life that had become dim and flickered many times had now begun to shine much brighter and illuminate new horizons. The wind of change was coming, its intensity growing ever stronger. I discovered concealed between the lines of the poem a fourth choice and its true meaning. It wasn't just about a physical journey but a spiritual one that would eventually lead to my final destiny. The spiritual overtone demanded consideration, and I would like to think Robert Frost knew exactly where the road he chose would eventually terminate. He chose the road less traveled. No one will ever know the mind of the poet, but perhaps his description of a physical journey is truly nothing more than an analogy of man's spiritual journey, which ends at the gates to eternity.

The writer drew a very close parallel to the two gates mentioned in the Bible, specifically in the book of Matthew (7:13-14). Matthew described these two gates as the small gate leading to a narrow road few people travel (the road less traveled), which leads to heaven; and the other is a large gate, which opens to a wide road many people travel (the other road), but it leads to destruction. Perhaps there was an underlying reason for him to choose the road less traveled, because it illustrates the biblical description of a narrow road that leads back to paradise, the Garden of Eden, and the Tree of Life. The other road represents the tree of knowledge of good and evil, which leads away from the garden to eternal destruction.

It was during one of my moments of self-pity when I discovered the broken bridges and damaged relationships I had suffered from were totally of my own volition. As I looked back over my shoulder, I was amazed to find that the foundation of the road was still solid; the surface was patched but still firm; the bridge structures were rusty but still strong. Their foundations were thankfully designed by my loving Father and built to withstand the test of time. I returned to my original point of reference—Mom and Dad's tabletop instructions. I switched from the "other road" to the "road less traveled"; then, entering through the narrow gate, I chose the biblical example of a narrow road, which was also less traveled. I immediately began to resurface the road and bridges with the love of Jesus Christ; next, I surrendered it all to the Holy Spirit to stripe and install the road signs, which I would need for guidance. I had made many mistakes along the way, but as is so often the case, the missed directions opened the doors of opportunity leading to second chances.

First, I had to turn around, go back, and remove the barricades I had constructed in my life. I had erected lots of them, and as I eliminated them one by one, I began to experience a new understanding of the true value of friends and relationships. I found that real friends tell friends the truth, regardless of the consequences. I had abandoned many of my old friends in favor of my new lifestyle. Now I would once again embrace my past and from there build new lasting relationships—those that would guide me into a happier and more fulfilling life. I realized that being less than someone expected of me did not necessarily constitute failed relationships or sever the bond we once had as true friends. I discovered that true friends are willing to forgive your mistakes and accept you just the way you are, then love you in the same manner Christ first loved us.

Simply stated, I realized that the fullness of life would be experienced only through a loving relationship with our heavenly Father and then shared in each and every one of life's encounters. I was still on the road to discovery, but the light kept getting brighter. The search for my road to paradise was finally coming into focus through the realization that only my heavenly Father knew the direction I needed to take, the length of my journey, the mountains I must climb, the disappointments that lay hidden in the valleys, the bridges I must cross, and most of all, the time of arrival at my final destination. I was returning to my roots, my default point of reference: the family circle and my tabletop education. I had learned from my mistakes and was now going to take advantage of the experiences gathered from along the road I had traveled. My heavenly Father now became the object of my dreams; I now knew only He held the plans for my life. "Do not conform to the pattern of this world, but be transformed by the renewing of your mind. Then you will be able to test and approve what God's will is—his good, pleasing and perfect will" (Romans 12:2).

I was in the process of developing a new way of life, one that would move the needle from failure to success by my conformance to this new set of standards. I was now building on my successes and failures, embracing a second chance I had been given, and blending them into a harmonious relationship with Christ. My dreams of discovering a road to paradise built from fame and fortune had crashed and burned. I was abandoning the concept of "The Road Not Taken" and turning to a new playbook for guidance, the Bible.

The Blender
Chapter 4

Love best describes the atmosphere that surrounded my mom and dad's home. They were a great team, blending their love for each other, their family, and their love for God; together they shaped what I look back on as the ideal family circle. They raised six wonderful children and lived to celebrate sixty uninterrupted years of marriage. Their family circle was made up of four sons and two daughters. I am sure I must have asked them ten thousand times ten thousand questions while growing up, but there remained one question I could never muster the courage to ask: "Was it fun raising us six kids?" There were many times when I'm sure they would have answered my sarcasm with something much less than a warm smile, and as I learned later, it would become a self-fulfilling question with my own family.

My parents knew how to make a house into a home. To me it was a place where I could unconditionally return to regardless of the circumstances that had separated us. So if home is truly where the heart is, what then molds the individual characters of a family into a unified family? It is so much more than the obvious. It cannot simply be contained in a biological capsule; it is the comfort zone that envelops parents and siblings, who live together in peace, love, and harmony. These are fundamental to an ideal family. Of course, harmony is seldom low-key or docile in a family with children. The more people living together in a small house with one or no bathroom, the livelier that harmony becomes. It is an environment that receives its life from the love, most of the time, and compassion shared by and for each other. Ever heard of sibling rivalry? But it is all about bringing the family's experiences into focus—into the center of the circle, and then blending them into one unified loving family.

There are many great rooms and special places in a home, but there is one favorite room that satisfies every person's soul more fully than all the others. It gives meaning and substance to the dawn and evening of each day in a way no other room can. I'll refer to it as the "Queen's room." Which room would you choose to fill this honored role in your home? My special place was where coffee, milk, juice, grits, fresh fruit, and occasionally eggs and bacon greeted the day. It was a place where our frustrations blended smoothly into freshly baked cookies and scrumptious meals. It's where a sneaky youngster got caught late at night, regularly raiding the refrigerator; of course, it was Mama's kitchen. Besides, it was equipped with all sorts of interesting gadgets and appliances. Not all were necessities, but even so, one of them was a standout; it even occupied its own little place on the counter. I think every kitchen should have one because it symbolically combines the family into a single unit while simultaneously lending a distinct flavor to the life of each individual member. Choose an appliance that lives on the kitchen counter, one that encapsulates the family circle, table, and road—an item that often produces surprises yet can be used as a very accurate life compass.

Which item did you choose? I cast my vote for the blender. As a young man learning to negotiate life on my own, you could say I took my life experiences and metaphorically blended them into a finished product. This produced the image I saw every morning when I looked in the mirror, and most of the time the one looking back at me was not always a happy face. The reflection I saw was the culmination thus far of my short journey through life. It offered little gratification but instead appeared as a huge door, open wide, and begging for change. Initially I had chosen the wrong road, the other road, but now as I perceived my life spiraling downward, my solution to this fiasco was simple; I would just dump all the ingredients of my life into my blender, relationships both good and bad, failures and successes, good days and bad, and happy with sad. The resulting concoction, I hoped, would lend flavor and variety to my newly created perfect living smoothie. In similar fashion, my life decisions, whether good, bad, or indifferent, would go into the blender, where they could also lend their weight to the final product. Actually, I anticipated something that mimicked the character traits I saw in my precious mom and dad.

I knew I had taken a majorly wrong turn during my first attempt at life on my own, having made lots of bad decisions that ended in miserable failure. Now, having gathered the residue from those past years and placing them piece by piece into my blender, I expected to discover a new and exciting direction for my life. I placed this blender in the exact center of my table, and after removing the top, I started filling it with every ingredient imaginable. The first to go in were my precious memories of the principles I had been taught by my family circle; they were my base and point of reference. Next, I added my tabletop education; it would become the catalyst for my new foundation. Then selectively I added some of my childhood pranks, a few things that fall under the category of youthful indiscretion and lots of other things that just simply defy reason. I also added some other things that had occurred along the treacherous road I had been traveling.

The blender was much too small to hold all the stuff I had experienced in my life, so I prioritized and topped it off with just a pinch of this and a dab of that—mostly minor mishaps that had occurred along my way. I weighed those things that still pinged my conscience. One particular incidence had occurred when we around three and five years old, my older sister and I poured a gallon container of cane syrup into our parents' bed; and then to make matters worse, we played in it, spreading syrup everywhere. Perhaps it was a childish fetish but Mom's bed held a special attraction to us. On another occasion, we raided her makeup cabinet, used lipstick along with all the other colorful items we could find, and painted her bed sheets. We thought it was beautiful, but needless to say, neither Mom nor Dad had the slightest appreciation for abstract art. I still don't know what makes kids do crazy things like that. Then quite a few years later, there was the time I wrecked Dad's car. Other than an old farm truck, it was the only transportation our family had. This too ended badly, a bad day for me, since we lived on a small farm about thirty miles from town. The entire event was a double whammy for me because the car was badly damaged and took about three months to complete repairs. Dad's initial response wasn't consolation or even a question as to whether I was hurt; he just stared at me in silence and walked away. His expression told me how deeply disappointed he was. I'm not sure he ever completely forgave me for that snafu, so I made sure this one went into the blender.

The next ingredient was a note of thanksgiving. It was all about the chicken and the BB gun. I was so relieved because Dad never found another BB in a piece of mom's fried chicken. Was I thankful? You bet, because if he had found one, it would have resulted in a near-death sentence for my younger brother and me.

The blender was almost full, so I only had to top it off with some special events I had experienced along my ricocheting road. To build a new road on a firm foundation, I had to retrace my steps, remove lots of barricades, rebuild some damaged relationships, and repair several bridges. One bridge I couldn't repair stemmed from my immaturity. I topped my blender off with the memory of my younger brother (eleven years my junior), who was killed in a horrible motorcycle accident at the age of twenty-eight. He was hit head-on one night by a drunk, who was driving on the wrong side of a very dark country road with his headlights off. This caused me to lament over the many opportunities I had missed to become more involved in his life but had not; these were little things that could have enriched both of our lives in so many ways. My take-away from our too distant relationship was this: it's the simple things in life that count, so make time for them. I forced my mind to reach forward, beyond the last mile of my brother's journey and final destination. I looked past the gate to paradise, the marriage supper of the Lamb, then to a time and place where once again we will join our hands in an unbroken family circle.

My blender was full to the top; everything else that needed to go into the mix would have to wait for another time and place. Since my blender was full, I was left with no other option than to put my loving Father, God, into a small box and set it on a shelf. After all, I still had the need for the freedom to make major decisions relevant to my best interests. Keeping God within arm's reach would also reduce the constraints attached to my life. After all, I envisioned my new self (the perfect smoothie and a new image of myself) working hard to disconnect from the evils of this world while engaging in good endeavors that would also be beneficial to others. Although I had accepted Christ as my Savior, I hadn't totally surrendered my life to His care and guidance. I was still clinging to the idea that no one could care for my well-being better than I could. So as far as the surrender to Christ portion of my life was concerned, I could leave that part closed between the covers of the Bible until needed. I placed the Son in the box with his Father.

I was now ready to start my blender, so with great anticipation, I secured the top and pressed the power button. With a zoom, it started with lots of clamor and clatter; then after several seconds, it settled into a steady whine. Once my new life was blended, I pressed the stop button and looked through the clear pitcher into its contents. I saw what I had longed for, a homogenously smooth-looking concoction, pleasant to the eye and jelled together into what appeared to be my perfect smoothie. From now on my life would be nothing less than smooth sailing. Finally I had connected all the dots and put all the pieces of the puzzle together. Now it was just a matter of appeasing my conscience by going to church occasionally, putting a few dollars into the offering plate, making a few apologies, and doing a few more good deeds than bad. In my mind this constituted a perfect blend for getting on with my new and improved version of life.

But when the blender top was removed, I was surprised to find that none of the ingredients had blended together as I had expected. The end result suggested that perhaps I needed to add more base to achieve a neutral mix. I would add some more of the good things I had accomplished in my life. Everything looked great from the outside, but the inside was disappointing at best. The little molecules hadn't interacted in the positive way I had anticipated. The mixture was granular with large, small, and sandy-looking pieces. They hadn't blended together, even after all my efforts. Every individual particle seemed determined to go in an opposing direction—a solution in total crisis—unstable at best. I ran it several more times without success; something was definitely missing. I added ice, hoping it would reconstitute into a uniform, silky-smooth solution but without success. Okay, if not ice, then hot water. Surely this would melt all the individual pieces together, resulting in my perfect smoothie. It still didn't happen.

What now? I've dumped all my life into this concoction, and not one piece of it served as a catalyst to the other; all those individual parts of my past were still determined to go in opposing directions. At this point, the why or why not didn't really matter; it appeared that I had taken the wrong road yet again—the story of my life. Perhaps I should accept the possibility that my idea of "my road to paradise" was, in fact, nothing more than a fantasy—purely an unattainable dream. My best attempt of what I had hoped would be an acceptable solution had backfired; instead of a new direction in life, it was quickly pointing me back toward my old way of life, the one in which I had survived many hardships but also experienced many of the good things life had to offer. But internally I sensed an overwhelming note of rejection; I knew in my heart that my solution wasn't acceptable to God. This empty feeling, the vacuum deep in my soul, was on a quest for something much greater; something that lay ahead, not behind.

By now I had poured every ingredient of my past life into the blender, expecting it to emerge in a shiny, new beginning. Unknowingly, I had overlooked a basic truth: "From life, come the things you have given life." In other words, from Christ comes life, and I hadn't yet fully given Him complete control of mine. I had chosen to place the Son of God in a box alongside his Father. My plan was to occasionally take the box off the shelf and release Him into my life on an as-needed basis. I consulted the appendix of my playbook, which is where I kept special plays designed for really serious problems. I sent Christ into the game for only these special plays, those that were too difficult for me to handle. I called on Him only after exhausting all my efforts and once again falling on my face in the mud. My selfish attitude toward Christ was faulty in every respect. This revelation annunciated my need for spiritual guidance that I knew must come from beyond my own resources and production. It had to come from the total surrender of my heart to the Father, Son, and Holy Spirit.

With the blender still open, I reverently removed my heavenly Father off the shelf and placed Him, along with his Son, Jesus, and the Holy Spirit, into it. I hoped that in spite of the wayward ways of my past life, they would accept me. Looking back, I really don't understand how anyone including myself could be so naïve as to think he or she could navigate the complexities of life without the help of Jesus Christ and the guidance of the Holy Spirit. I also added a splash of Pascal's Wager, along with my heart and the living word of God, into the pitcher. I sealed it up and stepped back, once again contemplating whether to press the start button. I knew that when I pressed it this time, my life would change forever. I knew God's plan for my life, a new life, would emerge and flow from that blender. Have you ever taken a glass and placed it in the center of a large, round plate; then mixed into the glass the appropriate amounts of baking soda, vinegar, and laundry detergent with water? The resulting chemical reaction produces fizz and foam; then tiny bubbles flow over the rim of the glass container and spread in all directions. The shiny, little bubbles fill the plate from the center outward until the entire plate overflows. The chemical reaction is the image of what God does when you let Him into your life.

I took a deep breath and pressed the start button; the blender began to purr. I watched while the barriers between all the granular and broken pieces disappeared. The particles slowly melted in perfect harmony into a smooth and unified mixture. The sound of the blender changed from a grinding noise to a smooth purr; this is the perfect analogy of the old man passing away to make way for the new. It is the reality of God's grace standing still and waiting for me to catch up. All the little molecules were finally attracted to each other; they were happy and getting along just fine. They seemed to be filled with love, joy, and peace. You guessed it; when the lid was removed, the ingredients that represented the purpose and fullness of Christ in my life began to pour over the top of the pitcher and into the plate, which then overflowed and covered the entire tabletop. It is unbelievable what Christ can accomplish with so little to work with. All He needs is the opportunity.

I realized from that time forward that I would need to look beyond the self-centered confines of my little circle and share my life with others. God took all the broken pieces of my life, and from them He created something wonderful, something good. He laid a totally new foundation by blending my weaknesses with His strengths. My priorities changed from "It's all about me" to "It's all about Christ and what He can do through me." His love migrated from that blender into a lifelong desire in me to share His love with others.

From my initial tabletop education, I had been taught that the Bible was a book written about the Father, the Son, and the Holy Spirit. I now hungered to know more about this Trinity, so I began to commit quality time to reading and studying the Bible daily. Through Christ's infusion, I could see myself turning from my old ways of life and miraculously emerging into a new person with a new life. My past failures were being overshadowed by this new concept, a vision of plans for a new road to paradise. This one afforded me the opportunity to share the love of Christ far beyond the shadow of my own life. It was a triple-good day! I had accepted the fullness of Christ and through my new playbook, the Holy Bible, I would discover the true meaning of what it means to know the Father, Son, and Holy Spirit personally. I also discovered that miracles are common to Christ, but they are uncommon and often unrecognizable to the world outside His kingdom; but I was the recipient of His latest miracle, salvation.

The Bible
Chapter 5

God, our heavenly Father, is the first person of the Trinity and absolute author of the Bible. This divinely inspired book, according to United Bible Societies, distributed an estimated 34 million copies in 2014.[1] It stands alone as the most widely distributed and read book in human history. I'm the proud owner of many translations of this cherished book. Most of them open with a tribute, acknowledgments, or other types of introductory statements. All these prefaces offer great scholarly wisdom and insight, but this one stands above all the others I have read. It embraces our heavenly Father's heart with a truly remarkable narrative.

> The Bible contains the mind of God, the state of man, the way of salvation, the doom of sinners, and the happiness of believers. Its doctrines are holy, its precepts are binding, its histories are true, and its decisions are immutable.
>
> Read it to be wise, believe it to be safe, and practice it to be holy. It contains light to direct you, food to support you, and comfort to cheer you.
>
> It is the traveler's map, the pilgrim's staff, the pilot's compass, the soldier's sword and the Christian's charter. Here too, Heaven is opened and the gates of Hell disclosed.
>
> Christ is its grand subject, our good its design, and the glory of God its end. It should fill the memory, rule the heart and guide the feet. Read it slowly, frequently and

---

[1] Rhodes, Andrea (2015, October19). *Record number of Bibles distributed.* Retrieved from http://www.unitedbiblesocieties.org

> prayerfully. It is a mine of wealth, a paradise of glory, and a river of pleasure.
>
> It is the giver of life, will be opened at the judgment, and be remembered forever. It involves the highest responsibility, rewards the greatest labor, and will condemn all who trifle with it sacred contents. (Origin unknown)

The Bible has the unique honor of being the only book ever written under the inspiration of the Spirit of God, the Holy Spirit. It is the only book whose words became fleshed out as Jesus walked the dusty roads of Jerusalem as the living Word of God. Its purpose is to guide the destiny of the entire spectrum of humanity. All who read it around the world are captivated by its central characters: the Father, the Son, the Holy Spirit, and Satan, their adversary. Although its words are especially sacred to the Christian community, many others read and learn from it also, grasping ideas along the way that hopefully move them past the brink of it being more than just a thought-provoking read, but that it would actually stir them into action. To all who believe and accept its tenets, it offers a cloak of life eternal through its central figure, our Savior, Jesus Christ. It is by far the only book of its kind. It encompasses the bookends of time, beginning with a fascinating account of creation and ending with a new heaven and earth, alpha and omega. Hidden between its covers and awaiting discovery is the mystery of the keys that unlock the gates to eternity. God wrote the Bible for a specific purpose; it was designed to direct the affairs of each of us as we travel our own road through life. Its intention is to bring every individual on earth into a right standing with God, to accompany every person along his or her last mile, and open the gate wide to his or her final destination.

To that end, AD 1454 was a good year for the Bible; it's the year Johannes Gutenberg mechanically printed the first copy of his famous Gutenberg Bible. Over the next 562 years, the complete Bible has been translated into 636 languages and has become both the most published and read book in the history of the world. It is most certainly the primary building block of the family circle.

This marvelous book was given to us as a gift from God and addressed to all humanity. It is a harmonious collection of sacred writings—living words designed to lead every person who reads it along a road of spiritual maturity, achievement, morality, understanding, and above all else, salvation. It was designed for the governance, consumption, and benefit of every aspect of our lives. Some read and accept it; others read and reject it; while for others it still awaits discovery. To a large degree, acceptance or rejection of the Bible centers on the premise of God as our Creator and Jesus Christ, the Son of God, its central figure. "All Scripture is God-breathed and is useful for teaching, rebuking, correcting and training in righteousness" (2 Tim. 3:16 KJV).

From beginning to end, all scripture is the inspired word of God. I've asked several individuals, groups, and even theologians the simple question "In your opinion, what is the Bible?" The responses I have received have all been very different, although all of them were very emphatic and highly opinionated. I was surprised to discover how many ways the Bible could be manipulated and appropriated to justify and support so many different lifestyles, especially as it related to one's own choosing. Among some of the answers were the following: "I don't know." "I don't believe in that stuff." "It depends on your religion." "It's classic literature, and anyway, I prefer nonfiction." Then there were those who simply said, "Who cares?" Others responded with, "It's a book of guidelines for living life," "It is a love letter from God," "It is the living word of God," and "It is the inspired word of God." Even though to me the purpose of the Bible is beyond doubt, the answer is always a personal one. To the non-Christian, the question is difficult, if not impossible, to answer. Clearly its acceptance and value to the Christian community were quite different from its rejection or pure apathy toward it by non-Christians. The controversy and array of answers surrounding such a simple question were incredible. Remember Pascal's Wager. "Either you believe God exists, or you don't." Since God is the author of the Bible, by association the same statement applies; either you believe the Bible, or you don't. Naturally, my favorite answers were, "It's the inspired word of God" and "the living word of God." Bottom line, there is no middle ground. It's not a restaurant menu populated with numerous choices, which allow you to select à la carte only those items that are compatible with your social status or taste.

To those who reject the Bible as the living word of God, it's just another book with little or no value outside its literary or historical contribution to the intellect of the reader. To those folks, it is widely unacceptable. It is counterproductive to relativism and doesn't support most of their culturally based traditions, and it certainly doesn't conform to or support the needs of our contemporary society. However, to the Christian community, the Bible represents the living word of God. It is sacred and precious to them, but at the same time, its truths can be applied to many things by many different people and in many different ways. Nonetheless, it remains the inspired word of God.

The Bible is a composition of sixty-six individual books authored by God, although selected men of God wrote it over a period of about sixteen hundred years. The thirty-nine books of the Old Testament and twenty-seven books of the New Testament were penned by more than forty different people, all whose social statuses ran the gamut from kings to tax collectors to fishermen. But authorship of the Bible nonetheless belongs solely to God. Here's why. Suppose you dictate a letter; your secretary types it and then returns it to you for your review and signature. Although you didn't personally type the letter, it is nonetheless yours since it bears your signature and conveys your thoughts to the reader. So it is with the Bible.

The Bible is divided into two parts. The Old Testament (OT) begins with the account of creation and continues from circa 6 BC to circa 4 BC, around the birth of Christ. The New Testament begins with the birth of Christ and ends around AD 100 as the apostolic period comes to a close. Together the testaments address every aspect of human life on earth along with a glimpse into our eternal future. Its pages ensure both blessings and curses respectively for those who accept or reject its instructions. In Genesis, the first book of the Bible, we are given an account of creation by Moses and introduced to our past heritage through Adam and Eve. It is often referred to as the "book of beginnings" and is the first of the thirty-nine books of the OT. For ease of understanding, these thirty-nine books can be topically categorized into four parts: law, history, poetry, and prophecy. Next, the Bible progresses to the NT, which reflects the heart of the Bible. In the NT God opens the door of our understanding and confronts us with our present circumstances. Our heavenly Father exposes our sinful natures and offers forgiveness through His Son, Jesus Christ. It becomes clear that Jesus is indeed the centerpiece of the entire Bible. The twenty-seven books of the NT are generally divided into five categories: the Gospels, the book of Acts, the Pauline epistles, the general epistles, and the book of Revelation.

The OT is often referred to as the Old Covenant. It lays a foundation for the coming of Christ through its laws, history, poetry, and prophecy; but as you immerse yourself in the OT, you discover God's promise to Abraham that he would become the father of many nations. The Bible portrays our father, Abraham; his son, Isaac; and his grandson, Jacob, as the seed of promise, from which His chosen people and a future Messiah would come. Jacob had twelve sons, and following their births, the LORD changed his name to Israel. Ten of Israel's sons plus two of his grandsons then became heads of the twelve tribes of Israel, God's chosen people. The tribe of Levi was chosen to serve as priests, and then Joseph, the remaining son, was given a double inheritance through his two sons, Manasseh and Ephraim. The Bible chronicles their tumultuous journey through time and the eventual growth of the twelve tribes into the nation of Israel. The tribe of Judah provides the historical setting for the future coming of the King of the Jews, Jesus Christ. The OT expresses expectations of His coming, but the NT provides the detailed history of our Savior's arrival and earthly mission.

In similar manner, the NT is sometime referred to as the New Covenant. It is generally accepted that the OT covenants passed away with the death of Christ, and the New Covenant was given birth through the resurrection of Christ from the dead. The old passed away to make way for the new. As the Bible transitions from the OT to the NT, it reveals God's saving grace by leading man from formalities, rituals, and sacrificial worship under the law into acceptance of His Son, whom we are now free to worship in Spirit and truth. The old tradition of sacrificial worship under the law found fulfillment in Jesus Christ; through Him the Bible was transformed into the living word of God and the source that leads the reader to a new way of life.

The Bible introduces us to the living word, which guides us to a better way of life that incorporates us into a newly found life in Jesus Christ. The Father portrays Christ as our Redeemer, one who paid the price for our salvation by paving the road of redemption with His blood long ago. From the beginning, He was the Word who stood by His Father's side; then the Word became flesh, and He walked among the people of that period on earth. He was crucified by His own people, died, and was resurrected on the third day. He ascended back to heaven to sit at the right hand of His Father. He is the Host, the Son of God, who will greet our heavenly Father's family circle at the marriage supper of the Lamb. The benefits of the Bible are too numerous to document and impossible for the finite human mind to absorb. But those who through faith accept its tenets will inherit eternal life. Those who choose to reject it will experience total separation from their loving Father, damnation, and an eternal home in hell.

The history, composition, and literary value of the Bible are beyond comparison, but the essence of this book reaches far beyond a scholarly endeavor. It teaches that we are beautifully and wonderfully made, created in His image for the purpose of worshipping God in Spirit and truth. Since God is Spirit and author of the Bible, it stands to reason that it can only be understood from a spiritual perspective. Therefore, the essence of the Bible is consumed and appropriated by us through the indwelling power of the Holy Spirit. Given this insight, switch the Bible as a book to the "Off" position, and then turn it "On" with the Holy Spirit as your Guide into the living word of God. The Bible introduces us to the Father, the Son, and the Holy Spirit—the Holy Trinity. The Holy Spirit is the voice and Spirit of the Father and Son. It is the Holy Spirit who breathes life into the Bible and serves as the key that unlocks our understanding of God's written word.

So again, what is the Bible? This question can clearly be answered fully only with spiritual understanding of its content and purpose. Without this, regardless of your answer, it is of little or no consequence. Let's backtrack to the earlier responses I received from my original question "What is the Bible?" Choose a response that easily fits into the anatomy of human emotions. Look for a key word, one that can both be given and received with equal gratification. I am going to choose "God's love letter to mankind," and here's why. The Father's letter, the Holy Bible, was written to give us purpose, knowledge, and understanding; but most importantly, it was sent to us as a marriage proposal. It is an open invitation to become the bride of Christ and then a member of our heavenly Father's family circle. Those who accept the Father's proposal are rewarded with the privilege of sitting with the Father of creation, at the table of the marriage supper of the Lamb. God's desire for a relationship with us flourishes through our relationship with Christ.

Although I have studied and taught the Bible for almost thirty-five years, I'm still not adequately qualified to answer the question, "What is the Bible?" Ultimately, it is a question that demands an individual answer. In my own life, I have discovered and experienced its fullness as the living word of God. Through reading, study, and prayer, I now understand what it means to have a personal relationship with the Father and Son, Jesus Christ. The Bible occupies a very special place in my life. It's not just another book, but it is indeed the inspired word of God; it is inerrant in every respect, and it serves as my absolute moral standard for living life. The Bible is also a book of introductions; God introduced Himself as the Father, Jesus Christ as His Son, and the Holy Spirit as our Comforter and Guide.

I founded and served as president of an electrical engineering and testing firm for eighteen years. One of my strong suits was writing testing and commissioning procedures for large national and international electrical projects. The engineering and testing came relatively easy, but for some reason I couldn't apply that same level of competence to understanding the Bible. I was accustomed daily to dealing with complex issues, but deciphering the Bible just seemed to elude me. No amount of reading, study, or research was sufficient to enrich my understanding. I had not yet come to the realization that since the Bible was the inspired word of God it can be understood only through the revealing power of the Holy Spirit. With this spiritual insight, I went directly to my heavenly Father's throne of grace, where in accordance with His promise I asked for the desire of my heart. I asked Him to simply "help me understand and appropriate the Bible to my life."

I don't recall the exact time or place, but extraordinary things began to happen. The Bible, like a bud with all its hidden secrets, began to blossom and unfold before my eyes much like a beautiful flower. As this flower opened to reveal its secrets, the words written across its pages were transformed into the living word of God. God had graciously answered my prayer, and the door to my understanding began to open. I realized that His grace was indeed sufficient. His grace stood in eternity giving me time to redirect my life. Suddenly I found myself reading the inspired work of God—His living word, not just another book. For the first time in my life, I was experiencing life through the eyes of the Son of God. I was reading the book Jesus's Father had authored. Wow! Now I could rest in the assurance that wherever life carried me, the Bible, the living word, would always be with me. It was now chiseled, written on the tablets of my heart by the very finger of God, just as He had written the Ten Commandments long ago and given them to Moses.

Now that the words of the Bible were taking on life through me, my objectives began to change. I abandoned my old way of life to go in search of a new life in Christ. My plan was simple. I would develop a disciplined reading and study program that would lead me through the 929 chapters of the Old Testament as well as the 260 chapters of the New Testament. In my zeal, I started by reading the first verse in the first chapter of the first book of the Bible. My plan wasn't about justifying my belief in God but confirming the statement I had heard all my life about the Bible being the perfect standard for daily living. I wanted to learn the true meaning of life, and this seemed to be the perfect way to embark on my new venture. I quickly realized that understanding the Bible is a progression. Every verse was dependent on the chapter from which it came to its associated book and then to the Bible as a whole. My pastor often reminds us that "It's all about context."

God's written word is indeed progressive and since Genesis is the first book of the Bible it seemed appropriate for me to begin my search for the true meaning of life there. One of the many distinguishing features I discovered about Genesis was its role as the nesting place for so many first mentioned topics found throughout the remainder of the Bible. These topics, mentioned first in Genesis, are critical to understanding the entirety of His word. The Biblical "Law of First Mention" emphasizes the eternal, unchanging unity and consistency of God's holy word, while providing a well-marked road map into a deeper understanding of scripture. The Law of First Mention states: "The principle in the interpretation of Scripture which states that the first mention or occurrence of a subject in Scripture establishes an unchangeable pattern, with that subject remaining unchanged in the mind of God throughout Scripture."[2]

The key words of a verse must be interpreted within the context of that verse. However, in most instances the preceding and following verses also serve to enrich its meaning. Also, since the Bible was written over a period of about 1,600 years the time of writing, location, and environment may yield a different interpretation, especially as you move from the Old Testament to the New Testament. Simple rule of thumb: Is the verse in which the word appears symbolic or literal? Then interpret, extrapolate, and appropriate. The Bible chronicles time from creation to present; yet it remains applicable to every facet of our daily life.

To enhance my understanding, I chose a study Bible that included notes and commentary. These added features enriched my understanding of the characters and character development. The notes and commentary also provided information on time, location, environment, and circumstances pertinent to the verse. Additionally, I found the concordance and cross-references to be very helpful in understanding the more complete message of particular verses. Please remember, the Bible's ultimate purpose is to bring everyone reading it into a right standing with God, which comes through His Son, Jesus Christ, the central character throughout the Bible. Among the many topics addressed, the greatest is the gift of salvation; this is the theme that marries earthly life to eternity and a heavenly home with the Father and the Son.

---

[2] *The Law of First Mention*. Retrieved from http://www.thelawoffirstmention.com

The Bible introduced me to the Father, Son, and Holy Spirit; even still, I have no concept of where my journey will carry me during the next five, ten, or even twenty-plus years. In fact, I don't even have the promise of tomorrow, but I do have an RSVP to the marriage supper of the Lamb. What I have gained from reading the Bible is the assurance that my heavenly Father holds the plans for my road to paradise, and He will complete to His satisfaction the work He has begun in my life.

The Father

Chapter 6

The story of a young soldier was told many years ago, an image of unforgettable tragedy (source unknown). Yet from his experience, we can see the analogy of a loving God, our heavenly Father, and His love for all of us. The soldier was severely injured while fighting in the trenches of World War I. His story penetrates the depths of agony, suffering, endurance, and hope; ultimately to find joy and contentment in the sound of familiar, approaching footsteps … Voices and the unmistakable smell of antiseptic, which mingled with the pungent odor of burned flesh, awoke the soldier. He realized he must be in a hospital. The room was dark, but he was confident the darkness would fade with the light of a new day. After all, he was not only alive but also apparently a living miracle. Day after day he had somehow escaped death through many months of trench warfare on the front lines. Just as he had hoped, dawn emerged into another day but not the day he had anticipated. Instead of seeing the beauty of another sunrise, dawn emerged into permanent darkness. He could not believe the miracle of survival had brought him to such a tragic ending. The light of day wasn't sufficient to penetrate the darkness of this strange, new world he found himself living in. He listened in silence as strangers' voices discussed how his eyes had been melted into their sockets by a flamethrower during a frontal attack by an enemy soldier.

He did not understand the conversation being held around his bed, but he listened intently as they discussed the moral responsibility of allowing him to continue life versus taking it from him. He called out, screaming in anger, but no one responded. In an effort to communicate, he tore at the sheets, kicking frantically, but the voices he heard nearby paid no attention to him. Then, panic stricken, he came face-to-face with the horrible reality of the dark world he was now living in, a world void of light and interaction with others. The intense heat from the enemy flamethrower had also damaged his mouth and vocal cords, leaving him mute. The extremities of both his arms and legs were severely burned and had been amputated. Now alone in his silent darkness, he found himself a prisoner locked in his body with nothing more than his thoughts, which he could no longer convert into words. His only connection to the outside world was through his conscious recognition of the sounds and smells of the hospital room. He was horrified by his inability to communicate.

His concept of time slowly developed, by listening to sounds of the opening and closing of the door to his room. He learned to associate doctors, nurses, and aides with the sounds of their footsteps and voices. Then one day the door to his room opened, and a stranger entered. He spoke with authority to the others about notifying the soldier's family of his condition and telling them he was alive. They also discussed making arrangements to send him to a facility closer to his home. Terrified, he listened as they casually discussed their plans for his life, plans unfolding with no input from him; they weren't at all concerned about his hopes and dreams. He had been in isolation with no visitors allowed since being admitted to the hospital. He finally became accustomed to the loneliness, but he couldn't bear the thought of anyone outside this hospital room seeing him in his miserable condition, especially his loving parents. Their last impression of him was of a vibrant, handsome, young soldier looking forward to a wonderful future after the war ended. He didn't want to subject them to the pain and emotional trauma of witnessing the destruction of their dreams by seeing his burned and disfigured body. He wished for death a thousand times over, but his physical condition didn't even afford him the privilege of suicide. His life's objective had migrated to one thought, a simple request: "Please don't tell my mom and dad that I'm alive." He was tormented with the thought of the doctor's plans to transfer him to a hospital closer to his family so they could share in the responsibility of his care.

The endlessly idle hours he suffered afforded him much time to reminisce and think of ways to establish a communication link with the outside world. Then one day after weeks of nothingness, a glimmer of hope emerged from his world of darkness. A mental light began to flicker; it started with a dim glow and grew into a brilliantly shining ray of hope. He remembered the communication skills he had learned as a soldier using

Morse code. Using head movements, the only part of his body he could control, he began to tap on his pillow the universal distress letters, SOS. He practiced the continuous string of three dots (S), three dashes (O) and three dots (S) almost every waking hour. From that moment forward, every time he heard footsteps entering his room, he started frantically tapping his head on the pillow. He knew a hospital environment was an unlikely place for anyone to recognize Morse code, but it was the only way he had to communicate. Perhaps he would somehow get lucky, but eventually he was forced to accept the inevitable; no one understood the special language he was speaking. However, in spite of its futility, he continued head tapping and hoping.

Then one day after what seemed to be a lifetime, he heard a stranger's footsteps coming toward his room. As the door opened to his room, as he had done so many times in the past, he started frantically tapping with his head. The room went silent; it was as though his world had stopped. Then the most beautiful voice he had ever heard shattered the darkness with a scream.

"He is not having convulsions. He's trying to communicate in Morse code," the stranger said. Finally, a dream came true; the doctors and nurses were talking to him and not just to each other. This was a good day! Over the next few days, he was told that his parents had been notified that he was alive and that he would soon be transferred to a medical facility closer to their home. He was neither asked nor given the opportunity to say in code (his newly found link to the outside world), "I don't want them to see me." So unwillingly, he reconciled himself to the fact that he would go with nothing to offer them but disappointment and the burden of his care. His great big heart was filled with nothing but love and compassion for them, because he anticipated the shock and emotional trauma they would experience upon seeing him in this condition.

With the transfer now complete, he found himself in his new home. Although his room was still filled with darkness, he could feel the comforting warmth of sunlight shining in from every direction. The muddy trenches, the smell of antiseptics, and the putrid smell of burned flesh faded into the atmosphere of his new surroundings. The air smelled fresh and clean far away from the cold, wet trenches he had lived and fought in for so many months. Being in a new facility, he didn't yet recognize any of the voices or footsteps, but mingled with the hustle and bustle of activity around him, he sensed an air of excitement. Then, as if on cue, the room suddenly fell silent.

Emerging from the silence, he heard the unmistakable sound of familiar footsteps coming toward his room. He recognized the cadence of those footsteps; he had heard them so many times as a child. They entered his room and stopped beside his bed. In silence, the young soldier rejoiced, knowing his loving father was standing beside him. Without a word or even a handshake, his father gave him the most precious gift he could offer: his love and a great big "Welcome home, Son." The family circle was once again complete. He had come home.

The beauty of this story is hidden within the heart of a loving father, who with great pride anxiously accepted his son just as he was. It's a perfect analogy of our heavenly Father's love for us. He embraces and accepts us without precondition, just as we are. After all, we are created in His image, the same spiritual gene pool. But more than that, our heavenly Father expresses and proves His love for each of us in an even more profound way. "For God so loved the world that he gave his one and only Son, that whoever believes in him shall not perish but have eternal life" (John 3:16).

But what kind of loving Father would sacrifice His only Son just for the sake of a relationship with us? It's a story that goes back to the beginning of time. It starts with the most beautiful and all-encompassing narrative every written: Genesis 1–3. The Father begins by telling everyone who He is. He introduces Himself to us as the Creator of the heavens and earth, the entire universe along with everything that exists in time, space, and matter. He is not only all powerful, all knowing, and all present, but is also the energy that fuels the universe—the power source that both sustains and drives all life. In His book, the Bible, He speaks volumes about Himself; but after reading it, you will most likely be left with more questions than answers. Questions like, "What is Your name?" "Who are You?" "Where are You?" "How can I know more about You?" "Can I have a personal relationship with You, and can You prove You really exist?" The list can go on and on.

Pascal's Wager in a broad sense engages each of these questions. He confronts the issue with the simple question of "Does God exist or not exist?" His wager addresses all humanity with one of the most profound questions ever asked. It is a self-fulfilling question; one that will ultimately be personally answered by the reader's chosen lifestyle. If answered correctly, it is a lifestyle that must reach beyond your cognition and terminate into full acceptance that God does indeed exist. The wager provides a solution to humanity's greatest dilemma. In true binary form, his proposition demands an answer of simply yes or no. Does God exist, or does God not exist? As an individual, you cannot travel both of these roads simultaneously, nor can you avoid choosing by remaining in the woods, as Robert Frost wrote. Neither can you ignore the argument by simply saying, "I don't know." The ostrich approach of burying your head in the sand won't work either; it is nothing more than a response void of understanding, viewed as a politically correct way of saying no. The question, by necessity, requires a definitive answer of either yes or no.

Blaise Pascal (1623–1662) wrote the famous Christian apologia, in which one finds Pascal's Wager. His argument of either God exists or He doesn't become self-evident when one crosses the border from life into eternity. If God doesn't exist, then you have nothing to lose by thinking He does. "If He does exist, then we stand to gain an awful lot by believing that He does, and lose an awful lot by thinking He does not. I should be much more afraid of being mistaken, and then finding out that Christianity is true than of being mistaken in believing it not true."[3]

Moses was a father image to the nation of Israel, God's chosen people. But Moses likely experienced emotional overload when God assigned him the monumental responsibility of leading His chosen people out of Egypt. His first directive was to address the children of Israel and tell them, "The God of your fathers has sent me."

Moses then asked God, "What shall I tell them when they ask me your name?"

God very powerfully answered, "And God said unto Moses, I AM WHO I AM. That is what you are to say to the Israelites: I AM has sent me to you" (Exodus 3:14). No doubt, Moses also, quickly found himself on a "Who is God?" learning curve. He undoubtedly saw God's true character and subsequently experienced His awesome power as much or more than any other person on this earth. Even though Moses is often referred to as a type of Christ, he could never physically or mentally fully comprehend the entirety of God. But through His written word, along with the ever-present tutoring of the Holy Spirit, God continuously enriches the lives of believers, just as He did with Moses.

God's attributes, some of which He has shared with us, bring into focus our heavenly Father's expectations for our lives. He takes from His infinite and unfathomable resources and then reduces them to a concept simple

---

[3] Jeremy Stangroom and James Garvey, *The Great Philosophers* (Barnes and Noble 2006), *Pascal's Wager*, 46

enough for human consumption. The attributes that are unique to God are separate from the ones He shares with us. His statement "My thoughts and ways are so much higher than yours" says volumes. He lowered Himself to our level of understanding, but He did not choose to elevate us to His level. Instead, of His infinite attributes He graced humanity with a select few of them; they now rest on a plane compatible with our cognitive ability. Both His esteemed names and attributes portray the inherent characteristics of our heavenly Father. It is through our knowledge of these attributes that we gain insight into the nature and character of our loving Father.

Unique only to God: He is sovereign above all, all powerful, all knowing, all present, transcendent, perfect, holy, righteous, eternal, immutable, unequaled, and just. Attributes derived from God and available to man are goodness, love, mercy, graciousness, kindness, faithfulness, patience, and compassion. How beautiful are the tender mercies He has bestowed on us? Not only do these offer a deeper understanding of the depth of God's love for us, but they also serve as the fundamental building blocks of our relationship with God, our family circle, and others. He wrote the program, installed the software, and designed it to be user friendly; it is more than sufficient for our needs. Our Father's program is available everywhere to everyone; just press the "I believe in Jesus Christ as my Lord and Savior" button, and it will download automatically.

Along with our heavenly Father's attributes, He also reveals His character through several different names. Each of these addresses different facets of His sovereignty and is unique only to God. The most prominent is Yahweh or Jehovah – I Am that I Am, a name that cannot be defined by anyone other than God Himself. It is the primary name of God in the OT. Others include Jehovah-Jireh – The Lord will provide, Jehovah-Rohi – The Lord is our Shepherd; and Jehovah-Shalom – The Lord is our peace. God is Spirit, but in each of these names, He represents Himself in ways that are applicable to every mental and physical facet of our lives. His names define Him as our sovereign God, I Am that I Am. His attributes identify our Father's character and open the door to a relationship and understanding between the Spirit of God and the spirit, soul, and body of man.

It is understood that both the sovereignty and true character of our heavenly Father are revealed in His names and attributes; but even so, it's only through a personal relationship and one's daily walk with Him that we truly come to understand the depth of our Father's loving care for His children. The transformation process moves from knowing about God into a personal relationship with Him, and then accepting the fact that a loving Father holds the plans for our life. I've been reminded many times through my life that I see only the forest, not the trees. The same principle applies to knowing God. There are times when we must go back to the basics and just accept and trust Him as our loving Father and His Son as our loving Savior; after all, the common denominator is simply stated: "God is love" (1 John 4:8).

"For my thoughts are not your thoughts, neither are your ways my ways, declares the Lord. As the heavens are higher than the earth, so are my ways higher than your ways and my thoughts than your thoughts" (Isaiah 55:8–9)....... "For I know the plans I have for you, declares the Lord, "plans to prosper you and not to harm you, plans to give you hope and a future'" (Jeremiah 29:11)........ "Trust in the Lord with all your heart and lean not on your own understanding; in all your ways submit to him, and he will make your paths straight" (Proverbs 3:5–6).

When I connected the dots (.......) between these verses, I realized I was reading a life specification, written just for me, that came straight from the heart of my loving Father. I not only saw the futility of my own plans but also realized that if allowed, God would incorporate His plans into every aspect of my life. "Trust Me"—that's all the Father was asking. Jehovah-Jireh, the Lord will provide. He would provide every resource required for the construction of my road—from the vision to the concept, specifications, design, and completion. In short, He would develop a complete set of plans for my road to paradise. The foundation would be built on a solid rock, laid in place by the hands of my heavenly Father. He would do all this just because He loves me.

The Son
Chapter 7

My dad was probably the first person I ever heard mention the Son of God. He introduced me to the name of Jesus Christ but not to the person of Christ Himself. A personal introduction was my responsibility. Since my life has changed and I now enjoy a close, personal relationship with Christ, I would like to introduce you to my friend through an introduction based on my personal experiences with Him.

I have lived and worked in Baton Rouge for many years now, and the commute from my office to many of my favorite restaurants and shopping areas has often carried me along a very busy Bluebonnet Boulevard. Noonday traffic, with its flashing brake lights, sudden lane changes, and car horns blowing, is the accepted norm. It is always chaotic because everyone is rushing to grab lunch, run errands, and still get back to the office before he or she is missed. Such were the conditions I was confronted with while waiting for a traffic light to change at a very busy intersection. I'll refer to this as "my bluebonnet experience." I'll preface this unforgettable experience with the following Bible verse: "Here I am [Jesus Christ]! I stand at the door and knock. If anyone hears my voice and opens the door, I will come in and eat with that person, and they with me" (Revelation 3:20).

I had surrendered my life to Christ much earlier, but it seemed that Jesus chose this particular day and time to drop in for a very personal visit. It happened while I was waiting at a traffic light; He spoke to me through the Holy Spirit and gave me a quick update on His storehouse of provisions. He said to me, "I knocked on the door of your heart, and you opened it, allowing Me to come in, where I took up permanent residence." At that moment, while stopped at the traffic light, the Spirit of the Son of God was so strong that it invaded my innermost being. The imagery of His presence was unbelievably real. In his hand He held a bag filled with stuff. He passed it to me and said, "This bag contains everything you will ever need in life; it includes joy in times of sorrow, peace in times of turmoil, a discerning spirit, wisdom in times of doubt, healing in times of sickness (both spiritual and physical), and guidance when you become lost and weary."

I didn't physically see Christ, but His presence was so overwhelming, and every word He spoke I understood. I knew I lived in Him and that His permanent presence would forever abide in me, but this visit from the Holy Spirit was like nothing I had ever experienced before. It was as though a long-lost friend just decided to stop by to say hello in a very personal and special way. It was an encounter with reality that now brings comfort and contentment to me every day, one that shall forever remain hidden in my heart. Since that encounter, along the way I've found numerous occasions to say, "Thank You," but I'm looking forward with great anticipation to the day I will get to say it to Him in person. All He ever asked of me was to open the door of my heart. I not only opened it but also removed the door from its hinges so it could never again be closed—not even in the most severe of life's storms. I expect the hurricanes of life will come and go, but that door will always remain open. I absorbed the whole bag of blessings He had assured me of amid all the horn blowing and unfriendly gestures. I may have missed the light change, but in that moment of time, it didn't really matter, since the light of Christ had just touched my life in a remarkable way. Like a prism refracts light, He illuminated every aspect of my life. The Light of the World became the stimulus that motivated my mind, will, and emotions. Summarizing, I could say it was a "really good day," but honestly, since meeting Jesus, all my days have been good; although, some were a little better than others. I discovered that it's the joy of knowing Jesus, the default, that underscores both the happiness and disappointments we encounter in life, regardless of the circumstances.

The Old Testament (OT) introduces the Father and then follows through with about 115 prophecies that introduce His Son. The prophecies and earthly history are fulfilled through Christ in the New Testament (NT). In Colossians 1:15–20 and Hebrews 1–5, the writers composed beautiful narratives that identify and clarify Christ—His superiority and the binding relationship between the Father and the Son. The writers both position and define the roles of the Father and Son by connecting the dots from creation to redemption. The Father's spiritual image is physically portrayed through

His Son and then revealed to us through the Holy Spirit. This Holy Spirit serves as our Guide, who then tethers us to the Father and Son's plan for our lives. Scripture records that His thoughts and ways far exceed our level of comprehension; we are commanded not to rely on our own resources and understanding but instead to trust in Him. He often overrides our personal plans by assuring us He alone holds the plans for our lives, plans that are given life through His Son, complete with every resource and insight required to bring them to fruition in our lives.

The Bible itself is a beautiful reflection of the Son of God, but to truly understand Christ's character, earthly mission, and eternal purpose, one must start at the beginning in the OT. I've already given my personal introduction to Christ (my bluebonnet experience) along with a reference to the Apostle Paul's narrative in Colossians. But a historical perspective of Jesus is essential to understanding how the Father merges His plan of redemption into salvation through His Son. In the OT, the opening statement of the Bible is, "In the beginning." God introduced Himself as the Creator of the heavens and earth. "In the beginning" is echoed again in the NT as the opening statement to the Gospel of John. John introduced Christ as the Word, who became flesh, the living Word of God. "In the beginning was the Word, and the Word was with God, and the Word was God. He was with God in the beginning. Through him all things were made; without him nothing was made that has been made" (John 1:1–3).

The statement "The Word was God" distinguishes Jesus from God while at the same time declaring Him in complete unity with His Father. In the beginning was the Word, the Son of God, not as a created being but One who preexisted and is forever established as an eternal being. He was with God in the beginning and is authenticated as the Son of God. These verses also suggest a visit back to the narrative of Genesis 1–3. Along with the account of creation, God also refreshes our memory concerning the tree of knowledge of good and evil. Adam and Eve disobeyed God and ate from the tree of knowledge. Because of their disobedience, they were expelled from the garden, which then by necessity made an imperative for the Father's plan of redemption. Enter the Son of God, our Redeemer. "For God so loved the world that he gave his one and only Son that whoever believes in him shall not perish but have eternal life" (John 3:16).

The prophetic insights that begin in the OT now come to life through the birth of Christ in the NT. "The Word became flesh and made his dwelling among us. We have seen his glory, the glory of the one and only

Son, who came from the Father, full of grace and truth" (John 1:14). They become alive through the Son of God, Jesus Christ, and the living Word. He was conceived in Mary by the Holy Spirit, and then through a virgin birth, He took on the earthly nature of man. He was born into a world of His own creation. Lots of new births were taking place here. It was a miraculous conception and birth, but His coming was even more significant. "This is how the birth of Jesus the messiah came about: His mother Mary was pledged to be married to Joseph, but before they came together, she was found to be pregnant through the Holy Spirit" (Matthew 1:18).

Have you ever been in a stuffy stable with poor ventilation, no air-conditioning, little or no lighting, and the scent of animal odors? At best, the conditions are usually deplorable and unsanitary, certainly not acceptable in today's standards as a maternity suite. For mother Mary, there were no epidurals or sedatives to relieve the raw pain of birthing baby Jesus. But don't forget, these were the circumstances of the birth of Christ. He was born in a stable, which probably at best was very similar to the conditions of the one I've described here. But Joseph was by her side through the birth, giving her comfort and support. "On the eighth day, when it came time to circumcise the child, he was named Jesus, the name the angel had given him before he was conceived" (Luke 2:21).

Jesus's circumcision, along with Simeon's declaration that his eyes had seen the Lord's salvation, confirmed and identified Jesus with Israel, God's chosen people. He also revealed Jesus as "a light for revelation to the Gentiles, and the glory of your people Israel" (Luke 2:32).

In Genesis, the Father prefaced creation with the phrase "in the beginning." The Son was with the Father in the beginning as the Word. Now, about two thousand years later, the apostle John echoed the same statement—"In the beginning." It was the beginning of a new chapter in the life of Christ—He, the Word, became flesh. Humanity was confronted with reality: God's Son in the flesh.

Now the book of Mark opens another chapter in Christ's life by once again announcing "the beginning." This book announces the beginning of His earthly mission, which was to teach the good news of the kingdom of God, the gospel of Jesus Christ. "The beginning of the good news about Jesus the Messiah, the Son of God, as it is written in Isaiah the prophet" (Mark 1:1). It was a global message spoken with a universal language and designed for the benefit of all humanity, the good news of the kingdom of God. But he said, "I must proclaim the good news of the kingdom of

God to the other towns also, because that is why I was sent" (Luke 4:43). Once, on being asked by the Pharisees who would come, Jesus replied, "The coming of the kingdom is not something that can be observed, nor will people say, 'here it is', or 'there it is', because the kingdom of God is in your midst" (Luke 17:20–21). It was and still is an entry visa to heaven, an invitation for all humanity to become citizens of His Father's kingdom. There are countless untold "new beginnings" centered on Christ, but the most important is the opportunity of a new beginning in Christ—salvation. His earthly mission revealed gave life to God's plan of redemption. His redemption plan was completed and authenticated through the death and resurrection of His Son.

Christ defined the good news or gospel as the kingdom of God, a kingdom centered in and on Jesus Christ. Citizenship doesn't require fanciful accomplishments, a passport, a visa, a vetting, or all the other nuisances associated with kingdoms of this earth. Instead it requires only one thing: belief in Jesus Christ as the Son of God and your Savior. "For it is by grace you have been saved, through faith—and this is not from yourselves, it is the gift of God—not by works, so that no one can boast" (Ephesians 2:8–9).

Moses, when introduced to God at the burning bush on Mount Horeb, asked, "God who are you?" In today's world, we are still asking the same question about Christ, the Son of God. We live in a Googleized, easy-access world, which continuously probes for the answers to our questions, questions that will satisfy the whims of our inquisitive natures. Google provides a platform for every addictive algorithm the world could conceive. But without explanation or clarification, God responded to Moses's question of "Who are you?" with a simple "I Am Who I Am." There is no more and certainly cannot be any less. If news reporters had been present, they would undoubtedly have said, "Please explain. It's vital to our listening audience. They demand an answer." But our loving Father saw value beyond our arrogance and egotistical, self-centered attitudes and graciously satisfied all our curiosities through His Son. His love, care, and guidance are sufficient in all things.

In the NT Christ enriched our understanding of His Father's name—"I Am that I Am"—by making seven "I Am" statements, which are found in the Gospel of John. Each statement is associated with people, places, and things common to that era. They are analogies associated with the culture and environment of that period, each with a heavenly meaning. They portray Christ in the unique role He satisfies in relation to the kingdom of God. Six of the seven statements converge on one central point, emphasizing that The Son is the only way into the Father's kingdom. The remaining point, "I am the light of the world" (John 8:12), serves to illuminate the path that leads to the border crossing into God's kingdom. Through these statements Christ channels the good news about the kingdom of God into one unified living body, the body of Christ. The Father's kingdom is populated by all who believe in Christ and accept His statement, "I am the resurrection and life" (John 11:25). His seven statements are the following: "Then Jesus declared, 'I am the bread of life. Whoever comes to me will never go hungry, and whoever believes in me will never be thirsty. For I have come down from heaven not to do my will but to do the will of him who sent me'" (John 6:35–38).

1. "I am the light of the world" (John 8:12).
2. "I am the gate" (John 10:9).
3. "I am the good shepherd. The good shepherd lays down his life for the sheep" (John 10:11).
4. "I am the resurrection and the life. The one who believes in me will live, even though they die" (John 11:25).
5. "I am the way and the truth and the life. No one comes to the Father except through me. If you really know me, you will know my Father as well. From now on, you do know him and have seen him" (John 14:6–7).
6. "I am the true vine" (John 15:1).

Each of these verses offers an in-road to a personal relationship with the Son of God, a relationship that culminates in the transformation of a physical body into the spiritual body of Christ. Each of the seven allegories serve as a spiritual receptor, the benefactor of man's soul. They serve as guideposts leading to the body of Christ and then to the Father's kingdom. I especially like the analogy of a gate or door because it's indicative of an entrance, offering all who pass an opportunity to come inside. I stepped across the threshold of that door and into the kingdom of God about thirty-five years ago. Since that time, the Holy Spirit has spoken to me numerous times in miraculous ways concerning my identity in and with the Son of God.

The Son's seven "I Am" statements portray Him in different roles, but each has Him standing between his Father and a sin-filled world. They serve as a paradigm shift that takes us from a world of darkness through Christ and into the light of God's kingdom. These seven statements are among the most sufficient and rewarding of all scriptures in the Bible. These "I Am" statements will ultimately serve to unlock the gates to eternity and forever unite or separate us from God. He makes it clear that no one can come to the Father except through Him. Also He says, "I and the Father are one" (John 10:30), then goes on to say, "I came not to do My will, but the will of My Father" (John 6:38).

These passages seem to represent two distinct persons with different roles; indeed, they have different roles, yet they are also one. While on earth, Jesus took on a physical body of flesh that served as an outer covering for the Spirit of God. God is Spirit and in the OT was separated from the people by a veil in the OT tabernacle, that was torn from top to bottom when Christ died by crucifixion. This torn veil now grants 24-7 unhindered access to God through His Son. The New Covenant portrays the earthly body of the Son as the covering for the Spirit of our heavenly Father, confirming Jesus's statement that "no one can come to the Father except through me" (John 14:6).

The occasional glimpses we have of Jesus's earthly journey as the incarnate Son of God help to bring His mission and purpose into focus, a mission centered on sharing the good news of the kingdom of God. As Redeemer, His purpose focused on building personal relationships with everyone who would accept Him. The good news or gospel of the kingdom of God was consummated through His death, burial, and resurrection. What happened on the cross didn't signify completion but rather the beginning of the Father's plan of redemption for His children.

From the time of Jesus's birth to His ascension back into heaven was about thirty-three years. He was approximately thirty years old when He began His earthly ministry (Luke 3:1). It spanned a period of around three to three and a half years. Throughout His earthly ministry, He preached the joy and happiness of the good news concerning the kingdom of God. He also spoke of the bad news concerning His betrayal and death. He performed many miracles, exercising power over sickness, death, demonic spirits, nature, and even the power to forgive sin. The Son of God did all this to emphasize the eternal benefits of our heavenly Father's kingdom. His message, ways, and works were all completed in preparation for the tragic ending of His earthly journey. All this good news and so much more filled the wake of His earthly travels, but it all ended with the sad news that His own people were conspiring to take His life. Jesus looked toward heaven and prayed, "Father the hour has come. Glorify your Son, that your Son may glorify you. For you granted him authority over all people that he might give eternal life to all those you have given him. Now this is eternal life: that they know you, the only true God, and Jesus Christ, whom you have sent. I have brought you glory on earth by finishing the work you gave me to do. And now, Father, glorify me in your presence with the glory I had with you before the world began" (John 17:1–5).

The bad news of the good news was that the Son of God must die—not because of any wrongdoings, for no fault was found in Him. Even so, among other things, the Jewish religious leaders found Him guilty of blasphemy. He claimed to be the Son of God. Their punishment for this crime was death by crucifixion. This method of execution was so cruel that it was forbidden under Jewish law, so they conspired to place Him under the jurisdiction of the Roman court. As custodians of Jewish tradition and law, the religious leaders concluded that it would be better to kill Christ than to lose the nation to Him with His message of salvation through the forgiveness of sin.

The conspiracy to kill Him was then set into motion. The Jewish religious leaders paid Judas Iscariot, one of His twelve disciples, thirty pieces of silver to betray Jesus. Following His betrayal, the Son of God, who knew no sin, was brought before the Roman governor of Judea, Pontius Pilate. After much review he pronounced that Jesus would be scourged, the most severe flogging administered by the Roman courts. Christ was stripped and then stretched between posts, where His hands were tied. The whip was designed with at least three leather thongs; each strand was approximately three feet long and embedded with lead balls and pieces of bone. The lashes were usually administered by two men, one on either side of the victim. The blows were designed to lacerate or tear the skin open, even to the point of exposing muscles, nerves, and internal organs of the victim's body. There was no limit imposed on the number of lashes inflicted on the victim; as a result, scourging sometimes even resulted in death. To further humiliate the victim, the brutal punishment was carried out in a public setting. Christ experienced both humiliation and unimaginable pain; He was mercilessly scourged. But the brutal punishment inflicted on Him was still not enough to satisfy His accusers. The Jewish religious leaders wanted more; they demanded His crucifixion. Although Pilate found no wrong in Christ, he succumbed to the Jewish religious leader's wishes, and then turned Him over to them to be crucified.

The vertical post of His cross was set into the rocky ground of Golgotha (called "the place of a skull"), a place of execution, the site where Christ would be crucified. It was located just outside the gate of Jerusalem. After the scourging, the horizontal beam of the cross, which could have weighed from 75 to 125 pounds, was strapped across His shoulders; then began His long, excruciating walk to Golgotha. Weakened to the point of exhaustion, He eventually collapsed under the weight of the cross. He tried but was eventually unable to stand under the load. The Roman soldiers then enlisted Simon, a bystander, to carry the cross the remainder of the route. Had it been just the weight of a piece of wood tied to His shoulders, Jesus could have climbed the highest mountain with ease, but it wasn't. Along with the weight of the cross, He carried the additional weight of the sins of the world, a load only the Son of God could bear. When He reached Golgotha, the cross beam was laid on the ground in front of the vertical post. Jesus was laid on it on His back, His arms outstretched and then His hands brutally nailed to the beam. His torn and lacerated body was then dragged across the rocky ground, hoisted up, and then fastened to the upright member of the cross. Finally, with His legs extended, His feet were nailed to the upright.

During the darkest moments of His life, while hanging on the cross in excruciating pain, the Son of God prayed the most compassionate prayer ever heard by the ears of humanity. While His executioners looked on, Jesus prayed, "Father, forgive them, for they do not know what they are doing." And they divided His clothes by casting lots (Luke 23:34).

I know it's a little out of context, but the request to His Father to forgive them is still very much applicable to the nonbelieving world in which we now find ourselves. His offer of forgiveness from the cross to this day radiates to all corners of the earth; the offer is continuously open to all who accept Him as the Son of God. His compassionate prayer of forgiveness and ensuing death was the greatest expression of love mankind has ever witnessed. Even so, His prayer has continued to often fall on deaf ears, and for multitudes, it continues to go unanswered. "It was now about noon, and darkness came over the whole land until three in the afternoon, for the sun stopped shining. And the curtain of the temple was torn in two" (Luke 23:45). And at three in the afternoon Jesus cried out in a loud voice, *"Eloi,*

Eloi, lema sabachthani?" (Which means "MY God, my God, why have you forsaken me?") (Mark 15:33–34).

We don't know, but could it be that for the only time known to humanity, our heavenly Father blinked, and the whole land was engulfed in darkness? The Father may have closed His eyes in despair as He looked on the world He had created, and for three hours the earth was dark because His chosen people, the Jews, had crucified their own Savior. The Light of the World had been for a moment in time extinguished; they had killed Jesus, the only Son of God. "Later, knowing that everything had now been finished, and so that Scripture would be fulfilled, Jesus said, 'I am thirsty.' A jar of wine vinegar was there, so they soaked a sponge in it, put the sponge on a stalk of the hyssop plant, and lifted it to Jesus' lips. When he had received the drink, Jesus said, 'It is finished.' With that, he bowed his head and gave up his spirit" (John 19:28–30).

It was finished. The sin debt was paid in full. Our Redeemer had paid an unbelievably high price. His body was removed from the cross by His friends and hurriedly placed in a borrowed tomb. The tomb opening was covered with a large stone and guarded by Roman soldiers; however, His death didn't signify the end but instead a new beginning. It wasn't about the stone that covered the entrance to His tomb or that it was rolled into place by man. Neither was it about the stone being rolled away from the entrance to the tomb, for it too could have been removed in the same manner, but it was not. Likewise, the empty tomb gave no clues, since the body of Christ was laid in the tomb by man; therefore, it could have been removed by man, but it was not. Man had the ability to take our Lord's life, but did not have the ability to restore it back again." The Jews, by way of the Roman courts, had killed Jesus, the Son of God, the Lamb of God, and their Redeemer. He had completed His toilsome journey from paradise to earth. After having walked countless long, dusty roads from the manger to the cross, now the Father, through His Son, would defeat death by His resurrection. Christ's earthly journey would culminate in His ascension back to heaven forty days following His resurrection. But before His death, Christ said, "The Son of Man must be delivered over to the hands of sinners, be crucified and on the third day be raised again" (Luke 24:7).

Our Redeemer, at the moment of His death, completed His prearranged earthly journey. Three days after His death, the supernatural occurred—He was resurrected. Beginning with that moment, the road of redemption was opened to traffic. A redeemer is one who frees or delivers someone from extreme difficulty, danger, or bondage by payment of a ransom price. The Lamb of God came to earth as our Redeemer, where He paid the ultimate price with His life and voluntarily paid the price for our deliverance from sin and bondage—redemption, meaning we were delivered or purchased for a price. It was deliverance with a price (Ephesians 1:7–14). Little did His accusers know that when Christ uttered, "It is finished," it wasn't the end but a new beginning. Yes, the stone was rolled away; not for Christ's benefit but for ours. The sepulcher was empty, and the risen or resurrected body of the Savior was gone. The Redeemer not only paid the price, but through His death and resurrection, He offered the greatest gift ever given to mankind—salvation—because He paid the bride's price for our redemption. The redemption road is the road that leads to His Father's house, the bride's chamber, and the marriage supper of the Lamb. The bride's price was paid in full and the road was now open for the return trip to paradise. His death closed the door to man's earthly physical relationship with Him, but then through His resurrection, He opened the spiritual door of opportunity that emerged into an eternal relationship with God—one that never dies.

Resurrected—Jesus was alive, and as Paul wrote in 1 Corinthians 15:6, "He appeared to more than 500 of the brothers and sisters at the same time." Following His resurrection, Christ remained on the earth for forty more days. During that time He continued to teach and prepare His disciples for the greatest task ever undertaken by mankind—to continue the work He had begun, that of spreading the gospel, the good news of God's kingdom. In preparation for the work ahead of them, He told them He would be leaving but would send them a Comforter, the Holy Spirit, an unseen Guide who would walk hand in hand with them along every step of their journey.

The risen Lord met with His eleven disciples in Galilee, in the mountains where He had instructed them to go. There Jesus commissioned them to now go and make disciples of all nations. He said, "All authority in heaven and on earth has been given me. Therefore go and make disciples of all nations, baptizing them in the name of the Father and of the Son and of the Holy Spirit, and teaching them to obey everything I have commanded you. And surely I am with you always, to the very end of the age" (Matthew 28:18–20). With His earthly journey nearing its end, Christ then commanded each of the disciples, "Do not leave Jerusalem but wait for the gift my Father promised, which you have heard me speak about. For John baptized with water, but in a few days you will be baptized with the Holy Spirit" (Acts 1:4–5). He then told them, "But you will receive power when the Holy Spirit comes on you; and you will be my witnesses in Jerusalem, and in all Judea and Samaria, and to the ends of the earth." After he said this, he was taken up before their very eyes, and a cloud hid him from their sight" (Acts 1:8–9). After He was taken up into heaven, two men dressed in white appeared to them while they were still gazing into the sky and said, "This same Jesus, who has been taken from you into heaven, will come back in the same way you have seen him go into heaven" (Acts 1:11b).

My heavenly Father laid the foundation, and now the blood of His only begotten Son would be used to surface my road to paradise. My road now led away from the cross, not a road that led to the cross where He had been; but by way of the cross to where He had gone. He left the cross and promised to go and prepare a place for me. I knew that God's plans and specifications for my life would be fulfilled through Christ's promise. He asked only one thing in return—that I believe and entrust my life to Him and accept His Father's proposal and invitation to the marriage supper of the Lamb. How could I refuse an offer so generous?

I had no idea what tomorrow would bring, but one thing I was sure of: I had finally discovered my road to paradise and the direction it would lead. I knew now that only the Father and Son knew the distance I must travel and the time of my arrival. I had no idea of the road conditions ahead of me, but for the first time in my life, I knew my final destination. I would never again, as I had in the past, lose control of my life because Christ promised us that the Father would send a Comforter in His name to teach us and bring to our remembrance all the things He had said. As promised, He sent the Holy Spirit to guide me along the road of life that lay ahead.

The Holy Spirit
Chapter 8

In the not-too-distant past, it was commonly accepted that we humans engaged life while employing only about 10 percent of our brains' total capacity. If this myth is true and we could somehow use the remaining 90 percent of our mental capacity, imagine the enhancements, opportunities, and clarity it could bring to our lives. Perhaps we do use more than once thought, since modern advances in medical science and technology support the idea that most of the brain is active almost all the time. But let's suppose the myth is true and that we in fact use only 10 percent of our gray matter. To what purpose then goes the remaining 90 percent?

God is Spirit, and we were created in His image, which means two things: God is the dominant gene, and we are created spiritual beings with a body of flesh. God further commands us to worship Him in Spirit and truth. Perhaps He is trying to tell us something; maybe He reserved the remaining 90 percent to achieve His spiritual purpose in our lives. So how then do we come to grips with an attempt to understand something as big as God? How do we tap into His overall plan as it relates to our day-to-day activities? It comes through the Holy Spirit, not in increments of 10 percent or 90 percent but in its entirety—100 percent.

Although God requires 100 percent of you, He still leaves you with 100 percent freedom of choice to live your life. God's design is complete both physically and spiritually, and you can live it to its fullest right where you were planted. Since God is Spirit, the 9:1 ratio of brain usage becomes a no-brainer. If our heavenly Father set 90 percent of our total mental capacity aside for understanding and processing spiritual matters, the remaining 10 percent must be for other stuff. He gave us the mental capacity and physical resources required to live a Spirit-filled life. But even within the Christian community, difficulty arises from our unwillingness to surrender even 10 percent of our lives to the Holy Spirit's guidance.

The Spirit of both the Father and Son is revealed to us in so many ways, all of which culminate in and through the revealing power of the Holy Spirit. In previous chapters I wrote about blending both individual and family values with the Bible—the living word of God. I also wrote about the Father and His only begotten Son and about how He became flesh and dwelt among us here on earth for a short period. Now we are going to leave that familiar landscape, dim the surroundings of their physical presence on earth, and immerse ourselves in their continuing work in our lives through the fullness of the Holy Spirit. We are going to tap into that mythical 90 percent of unused resources.

While serving as president of my company—and I'm sure it is the same with others in a similar position—I experienced the emotional roller coaster inherent in the business world. Internal and external obligations of the business environment continually presented a hodgepodge of complex propositions; exciting but problematic at best. My solution to those sometimes-bothersome times was quite simple: just call Mom. Mom knew little about the nature of my business, but regardless, she always had the perfect solution to my problems. Her answer was never, "I wish I could help," but inevitably, she left me with the impression that she was willing to walk with me hand in hand through every difficulty or tragedy life dished out. I'm sure she didn't fully appreciate the encouragement I found in knowing she was genuinely concerned for my well-being. Her willingness to share in my difficulties and suffer with me through each of them, regardless of the consequences, always offered the perfect solution to my problems.

One day while sitting at my desk and wrestling with some issues that seemed to defy logic, I reached for the phone and dialed Mom's number. I was greeted by a prerecorded message: This number is no longer in service. I suddenly remembered she no longer lived at that address. She had departed her earthly home to go and live with Jesus, there taking her place in our heavenly Father's family circle. My loss had certainly become heaven's gain. Although she will live forever in my heart, I will never again experience her reassurance or the comfort of having her take hold of my hand to help guide me through the pitfalls of my life. Her contributions could not be measured in terms of great or small but always in the vein of love and sufficiency. Now in the midst of my latest crisis, I found myself searching for something to fill that void. I desperately needed a loving, personal relationship with someone who would confront the issues of life with me—a person willing to accept me just as I was and walk beside me through all my encounters in life.

Then I remembered my "bluebonnet experience" and reached into the bag of stuff Christ had given me. There I found His promise. He had told me, "Never will I leave you; never will I forsake you" (Hebrews 13:5b). It was a promise He would now bring to reality in my life through the Holy Spirit. He began by exposing me to the source of Mom's strength. He explained that her strength had been derived from her personal relationship with Christ, a relationship driven and empowered by the Holy Spirit. It was a relationship that had embodied comfort in times of sorrow, guidance through times of confusion, and above all, the peace and joy that came from knowing Christ as her personal Savior. He reminded me that she had been a true role model and a living example of the building blocks I should employee in my life. All I had to do was surrender my entire self-100 percent to the guidance of the Holy Spirit. But as an immature Christian, one still growing in Christ, I didn't understand or fully appreciate the role of the Holy Spirit. Reduced to its lowest common denominator, it was simply a matter of faith and trust. I had accepted Christ by faith; now in similar fashion I needed to entrust my life to the supervision of the Holy Spirit and trust in His guidance. He would bring the Father's plans for my life into focus. He challenged me to reach for new horizons by living up to the godly standards my parents had portrayed in their lives and to depend on Him as a person of infinite resources, not just an occasional influence.

Since I was already a Christian, my next step was to pray, study, and question others in an effort to understand how to use and appropriate the active role of the Holy Spirit in my life. My curiosity brought me to the conclusion that the person of the Holy Spirit was one of the most debated and least understood topics in the Bible. His influence was accepted to varying degrees, most of which originated and were regulated from within denominational doctrines. My research revealed that there are an estimated twenty thousand to thirty-five thousand Christian branches and denominations worldwide. Their opinions on the role of the Holy Spirit in our lives vary within the boundaries of these various organizational structures. Within each of these groups, His position and influence does not come from disbelief but rather from scriptural interpretations or misinterpretations used to mold the doctrinal belief systems developed within these various Christian communities.

The Holy Spirit is widely accepted as the third person of the holy Trinity, but His influence is no longer considered relevant for many modern-day churches. Although I believe this to be a false belief, it is nonetheless prevalent in many denominations. It seems to be based on the premise that God's written word is sufficient for living a fulfilled Christian life. I contend that the Bible isn't sufficient; indeed, it is only a starting point. Its sufficiency and true meaning are deciphered only through the revealing power of the Holy Spirit, and only then does His written word become self-evident. The empowerment of God's servants by the Holy Spirit to perform miracles, signs, and wonders still applies to today's church; and yes, this includes speaking in tongues and interpreting those messages. While these hedgerows flourish between the various corporate structures within today's Christian communities, they should never be allowed to elevate to points of division within the body of Christ. Regardless of church affiliation, you must personally and corporately as a body of believers accept, experience, and entrust your life to the guidance of the Holy Spirit. Only then can you begin to understand and appreciate the blessings available from the Father and Son.

Following the resurrection of Jesus Christ, the Holy Spirit became the medium through which we now communicate with the Father and Son. He translates the Trinity's desires into a language we can understand regardless of our cultural background or the language we speak. According to the 2017 *Ethnologies*, the catalog of world languages, the earth's estimated population was 7.6 billion people and included about sixty-nine hundred living languages. You know what? The Holy Spirit is far beyond multilingual. He speaks every one of these languages fluently and can communicate effortlessly in each of them both individually and simultaneously. *Awesome* isn't descriptive enough! The Father tells us to place our trust in Him, to lean not to our own understanding, and to acknowledge Him in all our ways. Then He will guide our paths (Proverbs 3:5–6). These verses are brought to life when we internalize the Holy Spirit. He is a spiritual person who guides from within, not from without. He proceeds from the Father through the Son and then to us on a personal basis. I like to think of the Holy Spirit as our heavenly Father's communications director. He serves as our interpreter and spokesperson, who stands between humanity and God.

Earlier in my life, I had very limited experience in understanding or following the leadership of the Holy Spirit; most of my exposure came only by way of observation. I had often heard, but had no concept, of what it meant to live life "led by the Spirit." Surrendering to the concept of being led by any kind of spirit was so foreign to me that it simply wouldn't compute. At this point my life had been lived mostly on my own terms, but looking back at my past, I realized that Christ through the Holy Spirit had already been directing my life, even as a child. Perhaps it was at this current time in my life that I began to tap into that 90 percent of unused gray matter, because my cognition began to migrate more toward spiritual cognition and guidance rather than dependence on intuitive and subjective reliance—myself. The Holy Spirit reminded me that, among His many other attributes, He would also serve as my Teacher, Counselor, and Guide; He would walk with me hand in hand through every step of my journey. This was amazing, since I had been praying for God to give me wisdom and understanding so I might become a better servant. Now to my surprise, this still, quiet voice told me, "I will not only teach and guide you, but I will demonstrate what it means to place your trust in the Father, the Son, and the Holy Spirit."

As a visual, hands-on type learner, I wanted to see, touch, and feel the Holy Spirit in my life. The problem was I couldn't grasp the notion of being led by a spirit—something I couldn't see, touch, or feel, since it had no substance, shape, or form. I could associate my life with the Father and Son since they offered the imagery of human form, but the Holy Spirit was different. The third member of the holy Trinity, the Holy Spirit, was indeed very different. The Holy Spirit is the combined Spirit and voice of the Father and Son, and yes, as your life in Christ unfolds, you can see, touch, and feel His presence. An attempt to understand Him only through secular knowledge is fallacy; it isn't possible, since understanding comes only through a personal relationship with Jesus Christ. On my own I couldn't access that mythical 90 percent of gray matter, but Christ through the Holy Spirit fired up those little protons and electrons, and something phenomenal started happening in my life. Just as Christ opened the door of understanding of the Holy Spirit to the early church on the day of Pentecost, so it was in my life; the Holy Spirit began to reveal Himself to me in a very special way. He literally gave me a personal tutorial on the true meaning of "being led by the Spirit." I couldn't ascribe to His level, so He came down to mine and demonstrated His power. My trust in Him He verified, and my weaknesses through Him became strong. Again, it became a simple matter of faith and trust in the Father, the Son, and the

Holy Spirit; and as time passed, I began experiencing life more and more, led by the Spirit.

The mental representation I saw was not preceded by any physical, mental, or external stimuli. At first, I literally couldn't grasp what I was seeing. I didn't understand this imagery or how to interpret its presence. My heart told me it was coming from God, but my mind couldn't process it, although I knew it was significant and represented something very special. What began as a mental image developed into a beautiful burning flame emanating from what appeared to be the wick of a candle. The family of colors within this flame transitioned from a beautiful glowing red into the many descending colors of orange and then to a golden yellow, which then faded into bright white. The glowing colors radiated in every direction with perfect symmetry. The flame lived as the shape of a teardrop, poised on top of the wick of a candle. It never wavered or flickered but stood erect, burning continuously and carrying an intensely cleansing and purifying effect. The flame embedded itself in my mind so deeply that I could see it in every waking moment. It didn't restrict or impose itself on my daily routines, but I sensed a presence watching over every moment of my life. It was as real as the air I breathed; it was always there.

Its beauty was indescribable, and after several weeks, I did as I had done with my bluebonnet experience. I gave it a name: "my Flame." I prayed often, asking God to reveal its meaning, since it seemed imperative that I respond to His presence, but how? I didn't have a clue. After not receiving a clear answer to my many prayers, one evening while sitting at the kitchen table with my wife, I shared the presence of my Flame with her. I recounted every detail from the first appearance up to that moment. Before I finished, she looked at me in her wonderful Christian way and said, "Don't you see, it's the Holy Spirit? He is showing you something very special, and when He is ready, He will reveal its meaning." That was my inclination also, and she had just confirmed what the Father had revealed to me over the past several weeks. Now He was about to expose Himself to me in an unimaginable, unbelievable, and unforgettable way.

My Flame, the Holy Spirit, spoke to me! He expressed Himself in a spiritual language that defied interpretation, yet He gave me complete and perfect understanding. His speech was articulated through fluid, animated movements of the flame. The definition and clarity were so complete that they totally bridged the communication gap between my flesh and Spirit. He opened my heart and mind to understanding His language and method of communication. My Flame would nod up and down or shake side to side to indicate acceptance/approval or non-acceptance/disapproval. He would wave forward, backward, left, or right to indicate guidance and direction. His every move was situational and always fit perfectly into the circumstance I was in at that moment. He combined shape and form with movements of the flame to express His limitless attributes, all of which provided perfect interface to my intellectual, mental, and physical capacity. The 90 percent of unused gray matter had suddenly become dominant and had taken charge of the other 10 percent. I was given the privilege of choice, but sometimes He laughed at my decisions; in many instances, though, He gently encouraged me and led me in another direction. At times my Flame laughed or frowned, expressed happiness or sorrow, sat back and watched, or became passive and provided no input at all. Then at other times, through physical manifestations of warm or cold body sensations, He literally supervised other areas of my life.

One morning at about six thirty a.m., while on my way to teach a Bible study, my Flame displayed some unfamiliar and frightening emotions, something I had never seen Him do before. He became agitated and erratic, and then with lighting speed, He moved about in all directions. He was obviously disappointed with something that had happened; the experience was frightening, to say the least. It was scary. I was frightened. My first thoughts were, *what is He going to do to me? Have I done something wrong?* Within a matter of seconds, I scanned my brain but found nothing that should have offended my Flame. He sensed my discomfort and then just as quickly reached out and comforted me. I felt a warm sensation as though He had placed His hand on my head. His way of saying, "It's going to be okay. It is not you. Someone else has quenched My Spirit and offended one of my servants; you will go and speak to them!"

A few days later my Flame disappeared. He departed with no explanation and without warning. I went nuts; I prayed, "God what are You doing to me? Why have You taken my Flame away?" I had become so dependent on Him that without His counsel and guidance, I was utterly lost. My exuberance for life evaporated with the loss of my constant companion. Even worse, I felt that God had withdrawn His Spirit from me, that I was eternally separated from my heavenly Father; it was a totally frightening and helpless situation. I shared the emotions of my spiritual depression with my wife; while she had deep concerns, this time we found no answers.

While the mental turmoil continued, another image took shape in my mind. In place of my Flame, I saw the image of a ring of fire. The fire was burning downward while working its way around the edge of a circular-shaped object. It encircled the object with complete consistency and without interruption. I immediately recognized the ring of fire as the Holy Spirit, but He gave me no explanation of what I was seeing or what He was doing. I was still searching for my Flame and looking for answers while this spiritual roller coaster continued on its course. Mentally, I watched for several days as the fire burned its way completely down the object. Suddenly the object it encircled took on life; it unfolded into the reality of life itself, and once again I could see, touch, and feel His presence. The object was a person's head, and the ring of fire was the Holy Spirit, slowly burning its way down toward the neck and shoulders. I recognized it! It was *my* head—I was the object!

Astonished, I watched the fire of the Holy Spirit slowly purify and burn my sinful nature away, then replace it with the righteousness that comes only through Jesus Christ. The imagery of the fire burning down from the top of my head, across my shoulders, along my arms to my fingertips, through my torso, and down to the bottom of my feet was overwhelming. It was above my pay grade, way beyond my cognitive ability. The Holy Spirit had just revealed the spiritual cleansing and transformation that took place when Christ came to live within me and me in Him. I had searched for meaning and purpose to life in so many places for so many years, but until the Holy Spirit grasped hold of my hand and led me into the heart of Christ, I had not found it.

Words cannot offer an adequate description of the impact the Holy Spirit has had on my life, but through His teaching, along with the visible examples He shared with me, I truly became a new person in Christ. He carried me mentally from faith and hope to absolute assurance that my road to paradise would never again be in jeopardy. He verified the reality of my trust in Christ and then confirmed Jesus, my Savior, as the purpose and fullness of my life. True, our lives are purpose driven, but they shouldn't be driven by our selfish objectives but instead by God's plan working through us to accomplish His goals as we walk under the guidance of the Holy Spirit. Tutorship through the Holy Spirit taught me that yes, you can hear the voice of the Father when He speaks, and you must only listen.

Whether the 90/10 myth is true doesn't matter. He found a way not only to access and use that 90 percent of my unused gray matter but also to gobble up the other 10 percent. Now Christ has 100 percent of me, and we are both happy. The foundation of my road to paradise had already been built, the road paved by the blood of Christ. Now the Holy Spirit would complete the task the Father and Son had begun long, long ago. He gently but firmly led me into the plans my heavenly Father had for my life, plans that would carry me to my last mile and final destination. He interpreted and shared with me the desires of God's heart. He would lead me to the Tree of Life and the marriage supper of the Lamb, securing my place in the family circle of God.

The Teacher, the conveyor of the voice of a living God, had taught me well. Now He would test my faith by sending me on one assignment after another, all necessary stops along my road to paradise. I quickly learned to expect the unexpected; every assignment was above my level of spiritual maturity and usually stretched me beyond my personal resources. The challenges were never easy and from a human perspective often contrary to logic. I soon learned, though, to stop speculating and instead to approach these challenges with blind faith. Each was totally unexpected and came with no conception of the final outcome; but after its completion, I always glanced back in amazement and said, "Wow, I wonder how that happened?"

So, first and foremost, I had to learn to travel by faith; then upon arrival, doors opened, finances became available and vehicles were provided, along with lawn mowers and so many other things. Many times my assignment was teaching, speaking, praying with someone in need, or reaching out to a person with special needs. But in every circumstance, as God's plan unfolded, He not only provided the necessary resources but also through the empowerment of the Holy Spirit gave me the knowledge I needed to complete the work He had given me to do. So it was with Rose, Joseph, and Mona, all very special people God would place into my life. Through these relationships and others along the way, I discovered the true meaning of the tree of knowledge of good and evil and how that knowledge must be applied to the Christian way of life.

The Tree of Knowledge
Chapter 9

Construction was complete with all the road signs in place, so as I merged onto my road to paradise, I checked the day off as a "double-good day." For once in my life, I finally knew where I was going and how to get there. I was excited, but the answer to two really important questions still lingered in my mind. I needed knowledge and understanding of what God considered good and evil, those things deemed acceptable or unacceptable. My interpretation of this knowledge of good and evil would then serve as my moral compass. In conjunction with this moral insight, I could rely on the Holy Spirit to serve as my Guide for the journey that stretched out before me. This seemed to be a really good plan, but I quickly realized Satan didn't agree; he became very angry about my decision to desert him to become a citizen of God's kingdom. Since his first mention in the Bible, Satan has not changed; he still employs the same irresistible and cunning methods of deception he used on Eve in the Garden of Eden. You have probably heard the story many times of how he masterfully deceived her, and then both she and Adam subsequently ate fruit from the forbidden tree of knowledge of good and evil.

The tree of knowledge is first mentioned in Genesis 2:16–17. God placed Adam in the Garden of Eden as its caretaker. He told Adam he was free to eat from every tree in the garden with the exception of the tree of knowledge of good and evil. "If you eat of this tree you will surely die," God said to him. But in Genesis 3:1–7, we see how Satan deceived Eve by assuring her that she surely wouldn't die. She believed the lie and tasted the fruit. She saw it was good and offered it to Adam, and then he also ate the forbidden fruit. This forbidden fruit, off limits to them, was knowledge. They had disregarded God's command and were rewarded with exactly what they had asked for—knowledge of good and evil. Their acts of disobedience resulted in God casting them from the garden. They left the garden, wearing nothing but animal skin clothing their Father had made for them and the awesome responsibility of now having the knowledge of good and evil. Unfortunately, they gained knowledge of good and evil the hard way when they were expelled from their precious garden, the only home they had known. While in the garden, they had enjoyed only good; now outside the garden they would experience both good and evil. They were tossed out of their utopia and into the garden of life, where they would be required to sustain themselves through their own knowledge and efforts.

In exchange for this knowledge of good and evil, they experienced spiritual death – separation from God, which they enjoyed while living in the garden. Although they disobeyed God, He hasn't and will never remove Himself from the affairs of mankind. Their allegiance to Satan closed the gate to paradise and opened to them a new life outside the garden. Up to the time of their expulsion from the garden, they had been protected from evil and had experienced only good. But now they, along with all who followed them, would be required not only to choose between good and evil but also to live out their lives within the consequences of their decisions.

But why do you suppose Satan was so eager for them to have this knowledge? Perhaps he knew their pursuit of knowledge would become universal and radiate through the lives of every person thereafter. He also knew that having freedom of choice within itself would serve as a motivator to steer many away from God's plan for their lives. He rejoiced because the knowledge of good and evil opened wide a doorway for him to exploit the sin nature of man, thereby leading them away from the good that comes only through Christ. Satan knew that because of Adam and Eve's disobedience, all humanity would now be born into sin. Because of their decision to reject God, Satan had now gained ownership; he would no longer be required to take them from God. From this point forward, his goal would be to shield us from God with his deception, confusion, and the enticements of a secular world. He offered his followers the riches of the world with no moral constraints and even the self-denial that God existed.

But perhaps what Satan hadn't planned for was the second greatest gift our heavenly Father has ever extended to mankind, His grace. When Adam and Eve walked out of the Garden of Eden with the tree of knowledge, our heavenly Father spread His blanket of love, grace, and mercy over them and all who would follow. He did it because of His love for the universe He had created, especially His crown jewel: all of mankind. His grace and love are synonymous and have been extended to us without regard to worth or merit of the one who receives it. It is an expression of God's heart, which is portrayed through the person of Jesus Christ and then revealed to us by the Holy Spirit. This is a universal attribute of God, which is manifested in the salvation of sinners.

There was another tree in the middle of the garden along with the tree of knowledge of good and evil; it was a tree over which Satan had no control, the Tree of Life. This magnificent tree stood in the center of the garden and represented Christ, the Son of God. It stood in sharp contrast to Satan and the tree of knowledge of good and evil. These two trees were polar opposites spiritually, since one portrayed the image of eternal life in Christ; the other portrayed eternal separation from God with Satan. They represented man's first major moral decision, a choice to serve either God or Satan. Their decision made, God removed them from His presence and that of the Tree of Life, the presence of Christ. Our heavenly Father would no longer serve as the guardian of the tree of knowledge, but now He would place it squarely on the shoulders of all humanity, where it would become man's responsibility. On the surface, the privilege of having freedom of choice seemed to offer wonderful opportunities; instead of opportunity, it was a deceptively heavy burden, one that propelled humanity into a world of crisis. The world would now and for all time be a place in which every person would be free to choose right from wrong but then be held accountable for his or her decisions. God planned and directed the lives of Adam and Eve while in the garden, but He also gave them the privilege of choice, even while under His guidance. Given this freedom, they chose to plan their own lives through the understanding that the tree of knowledge gave them.

The tree of knowledge is on an equal par with all the other great teachings of the Bible. But when it transitions from the OT to the NT economy, it takes on a totally different meaning. In the OT, the Mosaic Law or Ten Commandments served as the dividing line between good and evil for God's chosen people. God used it to describe the results of cause and effect; good and evil was a precursor to the Ten Commandments, which were God's response to the sinful nature of human kind. In the NT it stands in direct opposition to Christ and casts a shadow of sin over all humanity. I searched for but eventually accepted the fact that our heavenly Father didn't provide us with a comprehensive list that separates good from evil. So then, where is the dividing line between good people who do evil things and evil people who do good things? How are these good people justified, and their good deeds found acceptable to our heavenly Father?

In the OT David prayed, "Teach me your way, Lord, that I may rely on your faithfulness; give me an undivided heart, that I may fear your name" (Psalm 86:11). As a maturing Christian, I asked God to give me that undivided heart, one filled with the knowledge of God; I also sought a discerning Spirit so I could correctly divide good and evil in accordance with His ordinances. I concluded that since I didn't have an all-inclusive list to follow, I could concentrate on pleasing God most by working toward the benefit of others. After all, if I committed some of my time to helping others, surely my heavenly Father would accept it and be pleased. It should be good enough! I began to commit some of my resources to that end. It was a great plan and one that would appease my conscience by satisfying the "good" component of good versus evil. This turned out to be a bad plan. I realized I was still on a continuously steep learning curve, and once again the Holy Spirit brought me face-to-face with another great biblical truth. The tree of knowledge of good and evil mentioned in the OT no longer applied; fast-forward to the NT and the New Covenant.

The first premise is, without faith it is impossible to please God. Next and contrary to the mind-set of many people is the fact that all one's good works are still unacceptable to our heavenly Father if we reject and deny Jesus as the Son of God. Even one's good deeds are counted as evil if he or she has denied Christ. There are no good works or so-called good people who are acceptable to God outside of Jesus Christ. Although my faith was firmly established in Jesus, I discovered that my focus was still partly centered on my own abilities and resources, not totally on Christ.

I came to another conclusion about reliance: Maturity in Christ is a never-ending process, and the continued guidance of the Holy Spirit is a moment-by-moment necessity.

Christ came to fulfill the laws of the OT and since the knowledge of good and evil was predicated, brought into focus through these laws, this knowledge too must find completion in Christ. In the life of a Christian, the OT economy of good and evil was neutralized by the sacrificial blood of Jesus Christ. The tree of knowledge of good and evil simply merged into the Son of God and emerged as only good, a product of His love and grace, which comes from the Father and Son. Therefore, since no one can come to the Father except through His Son, all good must consummate in and through Christ. "Do not think that I have come to abolish the Law or the Prophets; I have not come to abolish them but to fulfill them" (Matthew 5:17).

I then arrived at a critical point of understanding: All of my good deeds would never be good enough; they had to come through Christ and not solely from myself. "For whoever wants to save their life will lose it, but whoever loses their life for me and for the gospel will save it. What good is it for someone to gain the whole world, yet forfeit their soul" (Mark 8:35–36)?

It is disturbing to think about the eternal destination of countless great philosophers, philanthropists, inventors, and others who have made great humanitarian contributions to society but were and still are in danger of losing their souls to eternal damnation because of their choice to serve Satan rather than place their faith and trust in Christ. Under the New Covenant economy, the tree of knowledge of good and evil was replaced by the redeeming blood of Christ, so now we can become acceptable to our heavenly Father only through His Son. It's not a conscious effort of serving Satan but rather a decision of whether or not to believe in Jesus Christ as your Lord and Savior.

Knowledge is among the world's richest words, but if you look beyond its definition, you discover it cannot be captured or adequately defined, since it encapsulates not only time but also discovery, experience, and education. It defines both awareness and cognition, which apply to spiritual, secular, theoretical, and practical understanding of any chosen subject. The pursuit of knowledge contributes more to humanity's spiritual and secular journeys through life than any other single element. Christians strive to know more about the Father, the Son, and the Holy Spirit; sinners struggle to satisfy their appetites entirely through worldly endeavors. It is no wonder that God commanded Adam and Eve not to eat of the tree of knowledge. Whether you accept the idea or not, our heavenly Father knew knowledge was such an immense burden that humans could never harness or control it. Knowledge has propelled humanity from the depths of the oceans into the heavens, from sin and depravity into spiritual maturity in Christ. It will no doubt drive us into the jaws of Armageddon, all because of our inability to curb the mysteries of life, which still in large part lie concealed in knowledge yet to be gained.

Plato is credited with defining knowledge as "justified true belief." This definition gained wide acceptance in the eighteenth century, which history refers to as the Age of Reason or period of Enlightenment. Its influence is even more relevant today than back then, since it demands recognition of all humanly-derived beliefs. It justifies truth through intellect and knowledge; therefore, it demands that society accept greater tolerance. Now, God's absolute standard of truth is no longer acceptable to society while we dismiss all other perceived notions of truth. "Justified true belief" epitomizes the meaning of choice by permitting allegiance to either God or Satan; either is acceptable based on one's own interpretation of truth. In today's society, the doctrine of relativism teaches that knowledge, truth, and morality exist in relation to cultural, traditional, religious, and personal belief systems and is not predicated on the Bible as God's absolute standard. This doctrine closely parallels the idea of justified true belief. Although Plato's definition of knowledge allows one to choose— for example, between good or evil—it nevertheless places God's absolute standards of truth and morality on a level plane along with relativism and all other esoteric beliefs. This opens the door for one to know about God while at the same time allowing one to choose his or her version of truth and morality that over time becomes his or her norm for participating in life. This subtle method of deceit is Satan's most effective tool in today's contemporary society, since it allows one to justify and demand acceptance of his or her actions.

Knowledge can be appropriated in so many ways to so many things that even for a Christian, it is often difficult to draw a definitive line between the do's and don'ts encountered in our lives. Paul recognized the difficulties arising between spiritual and secular knowledge and clarified the mystery. "My goal is that they may be encouraged in heart and united in love, so that they may have the full riches of complete understanding, in order that they may know the mystery of God, namely Christ, in whom are hidden all the treasures of wisdom and knowledge" (Colossians 2:2–3).

I'm going to give substance and meaning to Plato's philosophy by blending "justified true belief" with my heavenly Father's absolute standards of morality and the mystery of knowledge hidden in Jesus Christ. The invisible God became visible through His Son, Jesus, only then was His truth revealed to us by the Holy Spirit, which is justification of my true beliefs. The treasure of all knowledge comes to us through truth that is found only in Him and there is no amount of good acceptable to the Father that does not come to Him through the Son.

Even though our heavenly Father didn't provide us with a complete itemized checklist of good and evil, in Paul's letter to the Galatians, chapter 5 contrasts the two opposing lifestyles. He characterizes good as love, joy, peace, patience, kindness, goodness, faithfulness, gentleness, and self-control. These are character traits that dress the body and should dictate the lifestyle of every Christian, for they are direct reflections of the Son of God. Paul refers to these character-building qualities as the "fruit of the Spirit." These examples only begin to touch the surface of the total Christian experience within the body of Christ. Oddly enough, these honorable traits also define the majority of non-Christians within the secular community. So where is the absolute dividing line between good and evil?

Paul advances both sides of the argument of good versus evil by compiling a list that governs the life of those who serve Satan. His list includes adultery, fornication, uncleanness, idolatry, witchcraft, hatred, variance, emulation, wrath, strife, seditions, heresies, envy, drunkenness, and reveling. These character traits, in contrast to the fruit of the Spirit, aren't compatible with a life in Christ. Paul writes that those who participate in these lifestyles can in no way enter God's kingdom. He refers to this incomplete list as "the acts of a sinful nature."

Ironically, the application of knowledge of good versus evil is that either of these mind-sets can fall under the definition of "justified true belief." So let's draw a line in the sand using the finger of God, a definitive line that indisputably separates the two. Either option, good or evil, represents one or the other of the only two gateways that lead to eternity. One is a narrow gate that opens to eternal life with the family circle of God. It is open to all who believe and accept Jesus Christ as their Savior and represents the good that is acceptable to God. The other is a wide gate, which opens to an endless life with Satan in hell—eternal destruction. It is open to everyone, both good and evil people who have denied Christ and because of their decision are serving Satan; therefore, all their good and evil deeds are unacceptable to God. While there is no finite list of "good one must do versus evil one cannot do," God graciously provides humanity with the mental and spiritual capacity to discern and choose between the two. Based on one's choice to follow either Christ or Satan, we each give God the indisputable evidence He needs to mark each of us as either a saint or a sinner, either good or evil; and then He rewards us according to our choices of words, deeds, and the lifestyles that we choose to live.

Remember that God is Spirit and therefore must be comprehended through the revealing power of the Holy Spirit; this demands a shift from physical to spiritual knowledge. Spiritual knowledge comes through Christ and is intuitive to the Christian; it is internal and must be understood from the perspective of knowing about both good and evil, not from a premise that good can be understood only through one's mental or physical practice of evil. Good includes all things that are acceptable to the Father through Christ, by whom we obtain righteousness and therefore right standing with our Father. The opposing side includes everything else, both good and evil. So should an increase in knowledge produce a higher level of tolerance in society? Certainly not, because there are still only two choices. If you haven't accepted Christ, you are on the wrong side of a very dangerous line; you are in danger of being rejected by God. Wow, I just used another few bytes of that 90 percent of unused gray matter.

Consider each of these three words separately: *knowledge, good,* and *evil.* Next, notice what Solomon writes: "The fear of the Lord is the beginning of knowledge, but fools despise wisdom and instruction" (Proverbs 1:7).

It is the hallowed name of God that Satan despises, the saving power of Jesus Christ that fools reject, and the instructions of the Holy Spirit that the lost world can neither receive nor understand. It is this Trinity—three in one and one in three, all in one and one in all—that defines truth and sets the standard for good and evil. It is this foundation from which knowledge is derived and the platform from which it is understood. Before returning to heaven after His crucifixion, Christ told His disciples, "I will ask the Father, and he will give you another advocate to help you and be with you forever—the Spirit of truth. The world cannot accept him, because it neither sees him nor knows him, but you know him. For he lives with you and will be in you" (John 14:16–17).

The Holy Spirit and the Bible are both the external and internal sources that bring to our remembrance all Jesus taught while here on earth; He continuously relays real-time messages to us directly from heaven. Christ is our only source of righteousness, but it is the guidance of the Holy Spirit that keeps us in a right standing with our heavenly Father. It is the Holy Spirit that reduces our understanding of good and evil to the lowest common denominator. It is the acceptance of Christ as our Lord and Savior, plus nothing. Everything else is evil and unacceptable to the Father. Again, the words of Christ underscore the fact that "no one comes to the Father except through me" (John 14:6b).

On a broad scale, *good* can be defined in secular terms as a response to circumstances, behavior, morals, measure of quality, adequacy, acceptance, and the list goes on. In the Old Testament, among many other uses, the word *good:*[4] Translated defines "moral excellence, benevolence, adequate, complete, serviceable, sufficient, and happy." In the New Testament, different translations define *good:*[5] "As a quality, either physical or moral: Beautiful, pleasing, useful, noble, or worthy in a moral sense." Step back from the various definitions and consider them within the following context: They all originate from the tree of knowledge, all of them denote worthy actions and causes, but outside the kingdom of God they are unacceptable in His sight. Why? While in the garden, Satan used the tree of knowledge to deceive Eve, and he is still using that same technique today. He is mimicking the beautiful attributes and goodness of the Father and Son as a cloak to cover his evil intentions, which will ultimately lead to eternal separation from our heavenly Father.

From the tree of knowledge, I discovered that life has numerous faces and wears coats of many colors, but even with all these differences, we all still have one thing in common; God is the maker of all. I also realized that with the passing of each day, the landscape of my life was rapidly changing and would continue to do so. The Holy Spirit was continuously implementing Christ's action plan for my life. I found myself on a learning curve that will surely continue into the last mile of my earthly journey. He opened my eyes to the simple fact that my good works alone were insufficient, that they must initiate from Christ living within me. My old nature of doing things my way to whom and when I pleased had faded away, and I emerged into a new person, one God characterized as good.

The tree of knowledge brought me to a face-to-face encounter with God's reality of life, a life that exhibits itself as an expression of the Father's love, goodness, and tender mercies. It is meant above all else to be shared with others. It is life lived out in a manner that truly exemplifies the truest meaning of good, the good that comes only through Jesus Christ.

---

[4] International Standard Bible Encyclopedia, (*Good, Old Testament*). Retrieved from http://www.biblestudytools.com

[5] International Standard Bible Encyclopedia, (*Good, New Testament*). Retrieved from http://www.biblestudytools.com

The Wine Glasses
Chapter 10

The wine glasses Rose gave me were beautiful. The bowls were fine transparent-red crystal and rested on clear stems and bases. A red wine glass often has a slightly larger bowl, with a longer stem than its white wine counterpart. The choice of color usually depends on the intended use, but the two glasses she gave me came without protocol or need for etiquette. After she left, I thumped the rim of one of the glasses; it resonated with rich sounds but not the high- frequency pitch one would expect to hear from expensive crystal. Even though her emotions told me the glasses were priceless because they represented her most cherished earthly possession. They were all that remained from a life riddled with cruel and unpredictable hardships. Had the wine glasses been valued in the millions, they couldn't have matched her facial expression as she passed this treasured gift to me. They were so special; I wanted to know everything about them, so I decided to measure one of them. The bowl was three and one-quarter inches tall, the diameter of the rim was two and one-quarter inches, the stem was three and one-quarter inches, and the glass was six and a half inches tall. They were designed for a three to four-ounce serving. Then, while staring into the empty bowl of one of the glasses, I realized it wasn't meant to represent origin, design, or monetary value; instead she was telling me in her own special way, "Take the wine glasses and use them to carry memories of me as you travel along your own road to paradise; they are the image of my love and the expression of my appreciation for you."

Roses are some of the earth's most beautiful flowers. A single rose in a lovely vase can express one's emotions in a way no other flower can. Its life begins as a small bud that grows and then opens into a beautiful flower.

As the bud approaches maturity, its petals begin to unfold from the center outward to reveal its inward beauty. Once exposed, its beauty is its sole contribution to life. After a time, the petals wilt, and one by one they fall to the ground, leaving you with only the memory of an act of gratitude and the image of a beautiful flower. The rose is certainly one of my favorite flowers because it epitomizes the joy that comes from giving as well as receiving—double joy. It encompasses the expression of love and gratitude. The life cycle of a rose is so reminiscent of my friend Rose's journey through life. A life may have grown from thorns, but its beauty became an inspiration to most everyone she met. One of my most cherished moments in life came when I was introduced to her.

She stepped across the threshold of my life through the compassionate heart of my office manager. She walked into my office one morning with a very concerned look on her face and said, "I need to talk to you!" Anxiety attack—my heart skipped a beat. I was afraid she was upset about something and was going to offer her resignation. Instead she told me the story of Rose, her next-door neighbor. As her story unfolded, I became increasingly sensitive to the plight of this German/Polish lady. I knew after the first few words that the Holy Spirit had orchestrated this meeting. It wasn't happenstance; it was preplanned, and my heavenly Father was placing it squarely in my lap. He was giving me the privilege of providing for her needs through the provisions He had generously blessed me with. Along my journey Rose was just one of many road signs posted by the Holy Spirit, which read, "Stop and lend a helping hand." Later I shared her story with my wife, and indeed, we did stop, but not for long. My office manager had no earthly idea what she was getting me involved in.

Her story began with the onset of World War II. She told me about Rose's experiences, beginning with the German blitzkrieg and subsequent invasion of Poland and how it had impacted Rose's life. She told the story of a little girl and how she had survived the horrors of war. At the time of the invasion, Rose had been a beautiful twelve-year-old girl living with her dad and stepmom in Poland. My manager shared the story of how her family home had been destroyed, resulting in their family being broken apart. Being separated from her family, she eventually found herself working on a potato farm in a German labor camp. As the end of the war approached, she managed to leave the labor camp and became a nomad. She now found herself living with other homeless people in the basement of a bombed-out building with little food or adequate clothing. Homelessness, hunger, and cold were the norm of her existence for many months. She spent much of her time begging for bread, waiting in food lines, and searching for food supplies dropped by allied relief effort airplanes. Life itself had become a daily struggle and fight for survival.

After what seemed like an eternity, the war ended, and she returned to an unrecognizable place, a place that long ago she had called home. The ravages of war had taken its toll on her family, but even so, those members who had survived were again united and determined to build a new life and future. During this period, she met, fell in love with, and married a young American soldier, who was serving with the Allied occupation forces in Germany. Later he was reassigned to duty in the United States, so with her only companion, her beloved beagle, she left behind family and friends and set sail to join her husband and find a new home in America.

The silver lining behind the dark clouds of her early years was slowly beginning to shine through. Fortune smiled on the newlyweds, and over the next several years, times were good. Her childhood dream of meeting and marrying a handsome prince had come true. After much hard work and determination, she also realized her longtime dream of becoming a US citizen. She enjoyed working with her husband, and together they were living the American dream.

Perhaps the problem grew from the residue of war, but as time passed, she watched her husband slowly become an abusive alcoholic. The incredible years of their wonderful marriage were becoming unraveled and eventually ended in divorce. Now in her sixties, she was once again alone, this time in a foreign country, and confronted with the awesome task of survival. She worked as a waitress for a while but lost her job due to a work-related accident. She was unable to find gainful employment once she was healed and quickly fell deeper and deeper into debt. Now confronted with a financial crisis, she could no longer afford the essentials of life; she couldn't pay her home mortgage, utilities, and other bills. Her electric, water, and sewer services were eventually disconnected; then to further complicate matters, she received an eviction notice from the sheriff's department due to missed mortgage payments.

She reminisced of her grueling days on that German labor farm and how she had endured so many past hardships. She thought about the many times she had walked across a frozen lake to go to a nearby town and beg for bread to help feed her and others in the camp. She had survived the bombings of

Berlin and experienced the beauty of a loving marriage, but now it was over, and she found herself staring at a mountain that seemed too steep to climb.

My office manager ended the story of Rose in tears. Her closing comment was, "Now she will be homeless again, and she cannot survive on the streets." She had no way of knowing, but only the Holy Spirit could have orchestrated the story she had just shared with me. My Flame, the Holy Spirit, my Guide, spoke to me as I listened and said, "The Lord has heard the prayers of His child Rose, and I am placing her care into your hands; her needs are now your responsibility." I had no idea where to begin, but I was certain He would give me a starting point and then guide me every step of the way. Rose would now be my companion as I walked along my road to paradise. I knew the landscape bordering my road was in for a seasonal change.

Leading up to this time in my life, God had prospered both my business and personal life. In my mind, I had arrived and was happily traveling along my road of paradise. Of course I was wrong, and once again I had arrived at the mistaken conclusion that I was doing everything right and living in the center of God's will; but as the Holy Spirit had done so many times in the past, He reset my priorities. He confirmed to me that indeed I was traveling on my road to paradise; then He made it abundantly clear to me that it wasn't due to my accomplishments but rather because of God's plans at work through me. I was reminded that my road to paradise stretched ahead of me and that He would illuminate the path I must travel. The little light in my life that had grown so dim at times was now shining much brighter. The glow had changed when I accepted Christ; now it was really getting bright—intensely bright. It was brilliant and shining directly on Rose. Earlier I had begun walking along my road to paradise; now through Rose, a beautiful lady with nothing to give but love and gratitude, I was beginning to discover the true purpose of my journey.

My office manager had no way of knowing, but she had just described to me the plight of a lost sheep, one of God's children whom the world was about to toss over the cliff. Rose's response to her circumstances was, "I'm just a little old lady wearing tennis shoes." The Holy Spirit had just given me the responsibility of bringing her back into the peace, joy, and safety of His sheepfold. Rose was one of the most challenging yet rewarding opportunities my wife and I have ever undertaken. As expected, her situation was urgent and demanded immediate attention.

I had just completed a monthly review of my financial statements, and based on a percentage of profits, I planned to make a contribution to our church, but something kept me from writing the check. Instead I asked my office manager to contact Rose's mortgage company and find out how much money was required to remove the eviction notice and bring her account current. They advised that her payments were three months in arrears and that stopping the eviction proceedings would require bringing the account current plus one month in advance. This came as a confirmation because of course the total matched the amount of the contribution check I was going to write to the church. I immediately mailed the check to her mortgage company. This allowed her to stay in her home a few more weeks. I knew it was a temporary fix, but it would also give me the window of time I needed to explore other options and also get her utilities turned back on. Shortly afterward, she got a job working at an antique flea market located on a large tract of land, where she soon became close friends with the property owners. It was a welcome gift from God, the opportunity I had been searching for. I spoke with the property owners regarding Rose's circumstances, and he agreed to let me park a large house trailer next to the shop if I agreed to pay for all associated costs as well as any future expenses. I was excited by his generosity and readily agreed to his terms.

My wife and I explained to Rose the benefits of living next to the flea market where she was working as opposed to remaining in her home several miles away. She loved the idea, and although the prospect was exciting, she saw it as nothing more than an unattainable dream. She simply didn't have the financial resources required to make this happen. She also knew she couldn't afford to continue living in her current home. She didn't know it, but she was in for a big surprise. My wife and I invited her to go shopping; she accepted our invitation, so we picked her up one morning and headed out. It was the greatest shopping adventure Rose had ever experienced. We told her she was going shopping for a house trailer that would be parked next to where she was working. She found exactly what she wanted and purchased a fully furnished twelve-foot-by-sixty-five-foot mobile home. Her cost was her signature. I hired a contractor to install all the utilities including central air-conditioning and heating. We located her new home under the shade of some massive live oak trees about one hundred feet from the antique shop. It was truly a beautiful home for a wonderful lady. She was well above being excited.

A few months after moving into her new home, her vehicle broke down. Her driving skills had gotten really bad (she was now in her seventies), so we decided it was best for all concerned not to have it repaired. Now without transportation, my wife became her default chauffeur. They went shopping every week, and my wife bought her food, toiletries, and other essentials. After shopping they always found time for lunch, often at the Chinese restaurant across the highway, Rose's favorite eatery, before going home. Of course the restaurant owner treated her like family too; she was so easy to love. As time passed, the shopping trips had to be combined with doctor visits. Her increasingly erratic behavior and signs of dementia sent us to a neurologist, who finally diagnosed that her irrational behavior was due to an inoperable brain tumor. A few months following the diagnosis, her illness progressed to the point that she became unable to manage her affairs.

Preying solicitors hacked into her bank account and every month with clockwork precision withdrew all her money. Her small social security check was auto-deposited into her checking account each month. The solicitors' checks were timed to debit her account, usually the day of or day after her social security check was credited. The solicitors' check amounts varied. The large checks hit first and then were followed by a series of smaller ones. The amounts were designed to ensure that all the money in her account would be withdrawn. If a check was returned NSF, they processed another for a lesser amount. As a result, Rose was robbed of her money month after month. The bank charged her NSF fees for all overdrafts, which resulted in her owing the bank more than $1,000 in NSF charges.

Out of desperation, Rose reluctantly agreed to let us manage her finances. We went to the bank with her and told them her story. The branch manager reviewed the account activity and very generously reimbursed her for the losses and canceled the NSF charges. She advised us to close her account and open a new one at another bank, which we did. Although we opened a new account for her, we couldn't give her a checkbook because inevitably she would give the routing and account numbers to solicitors, and the withdrawal cycle would start again. We put her on a cash-only basis, which she hated, because she was very much accustomed to managing her own affairs, and was determined to continue doing so.

We cared for Rose many years, but her mental condition deteriorated to a level that it became unsafe for her to continue living alone. She was one of the most independent people I had ever met; she vehemently rejected even the thought of leaving her home to live in another place. We prayed and asked the Holy Spirit to light the path the Lord would have us follow and above all else that Rose would experience peace and joy within the choices we must make for her. We visited several nursing homes in the area and finally found one we really liked; plus it was only a few minutes' drive from our home. We finally got up enough courage to ask her whether she wanted to go visit the facility, and to our surprise she said yes. We toured it with her, and while sitting in the administrator's office, my wife popped the big question to Rose. "Do you like it, and would you like to live here?"

To everyone's surprise, she said, "Yes, it is nice, and I think I could really enjoy living here." Another answered prayer! We drove back to her home and along the way discussed the plans and preparations for her upcoming move. She and my wife completed everything to her satisfaction. She spent her last night in the home where she had lived for the past fifteen years. The next morning we picked her up and drove her to her new home. She was sad but excited about the prospect of the new opportunities it offered. We visited often and provided everything she needed to ensure her comfort.

Rose emerged from the ashes of the most horrible war the world has ever experienced, then walked into a life once again filled with tragedy and misfortune. She spoke often of her family and wondered what had happened to them. Her greatest dream was to see her dad, mom, stepmom, and siblings again, but it was a dream that never materialized. She summed her life up with that simple statement: "I'm just a little old lady in tennis shoes, and that's enough for me." Her summation was such an understatement; she saw potential and opportunity in everything she encountered, since in her mind there were no mountains too high or valleys too deep; they were all just challenges to face and conquer.

I will always be indebted to Rose for sharing her life with me. Because she had shared the mountains and valleys of her life, the borders along my road to paradise had transformed into a new, colorful, and vibrant landscape. She taught my wife and me the simple truth that relationships come in many colors, but when seen through the eyes of Christ, they are all beautiful. She passed without fanfare, but her departure added another member to the family circle of God. I will see her at the marriage supper of the Lamb and ask, "How are things going?"

I'm sure she will reply, "I've been expecting you; I love my new home." She will probably add, "I have a brand-new pair of tennis shoes too!" Shoes are very important to one who has experienced periods of life without them.

Rose left her entire estate to my wife and me. The gesture more than exceeded the time and expense we had invested in her welfare over the past fifteen years. It had very little monetary value, but her legacy set a sobering example of faith, endurance, hardships, and suffering that was difficult to measure in human terms. She didn't see her misfortunes as sources of complaint but rather as doors of opportunity. Although it was only $800, she left us with an inheritance of wonderful memories plus a beautiful picture of herself with her precious dog taken just before she left her homeland for America. It still hangs in our home.

Lest I forget, the two red wine glasses she gave us still occupy a very special place in our home. When I take them from the shelf and look into them, I no longer see empty glasses. Instead, in one glass I find myself gazing at a profile of paradise. When I look into the other glass, I see a one-dollar bill; the two glasses represent the greatest value of all things on earth: love. It is what our heavenly Father gave us, and it's what Christ expects us to give to others. Again, it is a double-joy day that doesn't fade with time but lingers on to help chart the course of my life.

The One-Dollar Bill

Chapter 11

Monday was another one of those special days for me. My day began at five thirty a.m. and then a drive to Townsend to teach a Bible study group. Two or three of the guys always came in about six thirty a.m. and cooked breakfast for everyone. It was a very close-knit group of fifteen to twenty men from different area churches. Occasionally new faces would show up, and they were always welcomed with eggs, bacon, sausage, grits, pastries, juice, milk, and coffee. They were introduced to the group and extended a warm invitation to become one of our regulars. I attended this Bible study for about twenty years, and during that period of time, I saw many faces come and go, but one person stood out among all the others. I've labeled him "The One-Dollar Bill." This was the label I used to connect Joseph to my world.

He showed up one morning as an uninvited guest. After opening in prayer, I asked him to introduce himself to the group. He stood and said, "I'm Joseph, and I love Jesus," and then he promptly sat down. His short introduction was more than enough to welcome him into our group. We used the Bible as our text; our routine was to rotate reading the selected verses from person to person around the room. When it came to his turn to read, he stared at his Bible in obvious confusion; he struggled to articulate his sentences, stammered, stuttered, and finally with slurred speech managed to ramble through the verses. As he struggled to read, I looked into his face and saw the character of a very unique person—he was different. His set jaw and facial expressions suggested a person who had seldom been afforded any of the luxuries of life or the privilege of giving up and walking away from hardship or disappointment. He was a person whose determination had obviously overcome much tragedy and difficulties in life.

He became a regular and over the next several weeks shared many tidbits of his personal life with me. He had suffered a stroke, which left him partially paralyzed on his right side as well as gave him a severe speech impediment and minor diminished mental capacity. He also explained to me that he was paid a small stipend to maintain the lawn at a small business near his home, but his old push-type lawn mower was broken and could no longer be repaired. He seemed to be more worried about the lawn mower than about all the other problems that had beset him. I don't know whether I've ever spoken to anyone saddled with heavier burdens than those he was carrying. At the same time, I had never been acquainted with anyone who was shouldering the weight of so many problems with more dignity and self-determination than he was.

A few days after our conversation, I was in my workshop at home; and while I was standing in front of my workbench, the Holy Spirit spoke to me. Even though I still had moments of indecisiveness, I had become very dependent on the guidance of the Holy Spirit. He always expressed Himself to me in a language I could understand. It wasn't often, but occasionally He found it necessary to clarify His instructions to me. Sometimes with great authority, He would remind me, "I know your thoughts."

Today His message was clear: "Joseph needs help with his broken lawn mower." I understood. Along with other lawn equipment I owned, I had a small push mower used primarily for trim work around my yard. I considered what the Holy Spirit's had told me and made the decision to give Joseph my used push mower. It was getting old anyway, and this would justify buying a new one for myself. This decision seemed to be the cheapest way out, so I planned to bring it to him since I had his address.

Before completion of my thought process, the Holy Spirit, my little Flame, visited me again. He wasn't happy with my solution to Joseph's problem; it was much worse than getting caught with your hand in the cookie jar. His visit ranks very high among things I shall never forget. I was surprised by His reaction, since my motive was to help a new-found friend, but the problem lay in the fact that I was using Joseph's misfortune as justification for helping myself. Additionally, my solution to his problem wasn't sufficient to address his needs. It was an opportunity for me to dispose of some old equipment and in so doing give me a reason to buy new stuff. In my heart I knew it amounted to nothing more than a nice gesture, which was far from putting my friend's needs before my own. I also knew God had placed him squarely in the middle of my road to paradise for a reason, but I wasn't prepared for what happened next. I felt as though the Holy Spirit grasped me by the collar with both hands, placed His forearms on my chest, lifted me over the top of my workbench, and then pressed my back against the wall. He said to me, "When I tell you My servant needs a lawn mower, you aren't to give him your old worn-out mower and use it as an excuse to go and buy yourself a new one."

I knew the first moment I met Joseph that he was different, and as I had just discovered, indeed he was. He was not only a child of God but also one our heavenly Father seemed to have taken special interest in. The Lord revealed to me that since Joseph was no longer able to attend to many of his own needs, now He was giving me a portion of that responsibility. From that encounter I learned quickly that God doesn't accept Band-Aid or secondhand remedies to treat the needs of His children. He expected me to do the same for His children as I would do for my own or even more.

Without further hesitation, I went directly into the house and told my wife what had happened. She confirmed my thoughts with the simple statement. "Wow, God is so amazing." We both agreed that we would buy him a new lawn mower. I went to Sears and explained what I needed to an acquaintance who worked in the lawn and garden department. We chose one of the biggest, shiniest, and best-equipped riding lawn mowers the store had to offer. I also purchased a weed eater and gas can, along with some other items I felt Joseph could use. They would be ready for pick-up the following day. On my way home, I heard that quiet, gentle voice again. "He also needs transportation." Without question, I went directly to my office and unlocked the key box that contained keys to all my company vehicles. I took the keys to a red Ford utility van, pulled the title and registration, then went to a notary and had the title transferred to Joseph's name. It was a cargo van, well maintained and more than adequate to accommodate the lawn mower along with the other equipment.

The next day I picked up the new equipment in the van and drove to his home in Townsend. My wife followed me, and we both parked on the edge of a narrow street in front of his house. He saw us drive up and with a bewildered look walked across a narrow porch and came out to greet us. I hadn't visited his home before, and he wasn't aware we were coming. Naturally, he was curious about the reason for our unexpected visit. We talked for a few minutes, and then I asked, "Joseph, do you have a one-dollar bill?" He stared at me for a moment with that deer-in-the-headlights look, then stammered something like, "I think so." With that said, he went inside and came out a few moments later, holding a one-dollar bill.

While he was inside, I had opened the rear doors of the van and picked up a manila folder. The folder contained the title for the vehicle along with the owner manuals for all the equipment. I positioned myself in front of the open rear doors of the van so he couldn't see inside. As he approached, I reached out with my hand and asked for the dollar bill. His dark, piercing eyes searched my face for an explanation; he seemed to know something extraordinary was about to happen, but then he gave me the dollar bill. Before giving him an opportunity to speak I said, "There is one last thing I need." I then opened the folder and asked him to sign some papers, which he did. After signing the papers, he asked, "What have I signed?"

I told him, "Joseph, for the one-dollar bill you just gave me, you have purchased about ten thousand dollars' worth of equipment." Then I gave him the vehicle title along with the keys, the owner manuals for the lawn mower and weed eater, along with all the other miscellaneous items I had purchased for him. Then I asked him to look inside the van. As he moved around to the rear door, I said to him, "Joseph, you have just become the new owner of everything you see in the van, including the vehicle." I'm not sure which of us was the more excited, but he was certainly overcome with gratitude. Together we gave our heavenly Father all the glory and honor for the blessings He had so richly bestowed on both of us that day. It was a good day!

Meanwhile, back to my office, my lawn maintenance person was cutting the grass at my house with the old lawn mower. He called to tell me the lawn mower had run out of gas, and after refilling it, he couldn't get it to restart. I told him not to worry and to do the trim work; I would look at the mower later. A few minutes later, he called again to tell me he was experiencing the same problem with both the weed eater and edger. He had also refilled them with gas but couldn't restart either of them. He was a young man, who required lots of hands-on supervision, so I told him to put all the equipment in the storeroom, and I would look at it later. I was so glad I hadn't given these problems to Joseph.

I love to fry turkeys for ourselves and others during the holidays, especially during Thanksgiving and Christmas. I cooked them with peanut oil, which I stored in my storage building along with the lawn equipment. The peanut oil container was labeled and protected in a cardboard box and stored away from the gasoline and other equipment. I'm not sure how my lawn maintenance guy could have confused the peanut oil container with the gasoline can, which was red and placed near the lawn equipment, but he did.

You've probably guessed it by now. When I opened the door to the building, I noticed that the peanut oil had been moved. I opened the gas cap on the lawn mower first, and sure enough, it had been filled with peanut oil. The same was true for the other pieces of equipment. It was late, so I closed the door with the famous statement "I'll take care of it tomorrow." I love to procrastinate; it always ensures me of an optional starting point for the following day. Draining the tanks and cleaning the carburetors would be a great way to start my much-needed and anticipated restful Saturday morning.

Come morning I went back to the storage building and found the lock broken and door standing open. I knew I had locked it the evening before, so I expected the worst. Sure enough, I looked inside and discovered that my lawn mower, weed eater, and edger had all been stolen. Humorous yet still depressing! Undoubtedly the Holy Spirit was teaching me another great lesson. "When I assign you a job, do it right, or I will take away, even that which I have already blessed you with." I love the way God works; He truly does accomplish His will in strange and often mysterious ways. Ironically, in this case He took my worn-out lawn equipment and rendered it unserviceable, then had a thief come in the darkness of night to steal it. That's pretty comical when I look back at it. I was now given a reason to buy new lawn equipment for myself, but only on His terms. I would love to have seen the look on the thief's face when he found that none of the equipment he had stolen was in working order. I didn't share this incident with my friend Joseph, although he probably would have smiled and said, "God sure does things in strange ways."

Intriguing is perhaps the best word to explain my reaction to Joseph's request one Monday morning; he asked if he could open the Bible study with a customary prayer. I said yes, not knowing what to expect since he had a pretty severe speech impediment. But when he began to pray, his voice became crystal clear. You could hear every syllable; it sounded as though he were reciting the lyrics of a beautiful hymn with the vocals of an angel. He prayed with a beautiful baritone voice in prayer language that was strange to many of the ears in our Bible study. I don't believe anyone in the group realized that we had just witnessed a miracle. Even so, it was among the most beautiful prayers I have ever heard; it went directly from him to our heavenly Father's throne of grace. It was quite obvious that even with all his mental and physical problems, he was a chosen vessel, set aside from the world for the service of our Lord. Yes, he was wonderfully different. He was well established on his road to paradise.

Joseph is the object of my reference to the erratic behavior of my Flame, which I experienced in Chapter 8. No one in the Bible study group ever brought Joseph's commitment to Christ into question. Everyone loved him as his brother in Christ, but some in the group felt uncomfortable when he prayed in the Spirit. To address their concerns, I shared these words with them—words the Holy Spirit had given me. Prayer is a God-given privilege to mankind whereby we can communicate or pray directly to our heavenly Father. Prayer language is the Holy Spirit speaking through an individual directly to God and doesn't require interpretation, since it is one-on-one, man to God. Although the person praying is communicating directly with our heavenly Father, others who are listening can also be blessed and encouraged by his or her prayer. On the other hand, the Bible is very clear concerning messages and prophecies given in tongues to the church; these do require an interpreter. Again, prayer is the voice of a servant intended for the ears of his or her heavenly Father, the one who has the power to answer prayers. Whether we hear these words with understanding or lack of understanding doesn't really matter since we don't have the power to answer his or her prayer. Only God can provide for the needs of His servants. Although my explanation was well received, some felt it was best if Joseph wasn't asked to pray in the future. Everyone in the group loved him, but due to denominational exposure, some weren't comfortable with him praying in a prayer language. Although he wasn't present during our discussion, no one had to tell him; the Holy Spirit had already revealed the news to him. He was hurt and offended; the Holy Spirit of God had been quenched.

Joseph didn't return for several weeks, but one Monday morning, he visited us again. After dismissing the group and everyone was gone, I locked the door. The upstairs room where we met was in a two-story building with a narrow veranda running the length of the building, and on either end was a stairway leading down to the parking lot. As I was leaving, I looked back and saw Joseph sitting on the top step of the stairs at the other end of the building, his head resting in his hands. I knew something was dreadfully wrong.

He was my friend, and I could sense the deep hurt he was experiencing.

I walked over, sat down beside him, and noticed he was crying. We talked about the things that had transpired in the Bible study. He wanted so much to read and speak with clarity, but because of the stroke he could not. But amazingly, when he prayed, his words were clear and powerful. I loved to hear him pray; it was like being on the front-row seat, listening to someone speaking directly to God. Finally, he looked at me with tears in his eyes and said, "They just don't understand." That was the last time I saw Joseph and the last words I heard him speak.

The one-dollar bill he had given me for the lawn equipment now occupies a very special place in my home. It rests in one of the red wine glasses my friend Rose gave to my wife and me. The two glasses sit side by side and serve as reminders of treasures laid up in heaven. Joseph walked with me for only a short distance, but during that period he too dressed the landscape along the borders of my road to paradise. He dressed it with memories I will carry to eternity. Who knows, he may be seated across from me at the table of the marriage supper of the Lamb. It would come as no surprise to me if he asked, "Do you still have the one-dollar bill I gave you?"

I will respond, "No, Joseph, the Lord wouldn't let me bring it; it has no value here. Besides, I'm sure you've noticed that the streets of heaven are paved with gold."

Joseph enriched my life in so many ways. He taught me that only my relationship with Christ and others has heavenly value and that material wealth is only one of many different kinds of stepping-stones our heavenly Father uses to help build our road to paradise.

The Beautician

Chapter 12

Beauticians have the benefit of having some pretty imposing privileges. As their title implies, they are beautifiers, even though they often have very little to work with. Most all of them have captivating personalities and are great conversationalists; all of which are wonderful qualities. Once they seat you, they usually begin the beautification process by running their fingers through your hair and then asking, "How would you like it cut?" When they finish with their cutting and trimming, they always step back with pride, admire their work, and exclaim, "Wow, you look so nice!" I have never been able to determine whether they are admiring their handiwork, complementing the person seated in front of them, or politely asking for a gratuity. This is a lofty conclusion, but you almost always leave the shop refreshed and wearing a newly handcrafted image of yourself. I'm not a storyteller. I'm much better as a listener, so I prefer occupying my time while in the chair with my own thoughts as I await their parting words. "How does that look?"

Normally I give the beautician a tip, say, "Thank you," and walk away; but on this occasion I heard a story that demanded some immediate and serious follow-up, so I asked the beautician whether she would meet me later that afternoon. She said yes.

I enjoy the feeling of a fresh haircut, but as a student of good time management, I choose to limit the amount of time I lend to this unproductive activity. My knowledge of arithmetic tells me that the total time needed for my haircut, including travel, should be no more than thirty minutes per session. One per month would be sufficient, resulting in a time allotment of six hours per year. Basing this equation on a need-a-haircut life span of about seventy-four years, the total time spent would be roughly 444 hours at a total cost of about $17,760. In my opinion this is an excessive amount of time and money to spend on nothing more than conformance to the acceptable whims of society. Maybe our younger generation has the right idea; shave your head or let it grow. It's not the beautician's fault, but this amount of time is certainly enough to justify my procrastination.

I was scheduled to attend a project meeting at a large industrial plant in our area, and I was at least one-half inch overdue a visit to the local barber. As a matter of fact, my wife had already served notice that if I didn't get a haircut soon, I would be wearing a collar around my neck and sleeping in the little house out back with the small door in front; in other words I would be relegated to the doghouse. The decision was made. I would get a haircut prior to my meeting and certainly before returning home that evening.

There was a large shopping mall and several smaller strip shopping centers conveniently located within a few minutes from my office. No shopping center is complete without beauty salons with catchy names such as I'll Kutcha, Sassy Scissors, Magic Clippers, and so forth. I was encroaching on my thirty-minute allowance for a haircut, so I quickly packed my briefcase with the documentation needed for my meeting and took off. I drove from my office to a small beauty salon I had frequented a few times in the past. Opening the door, I immediately noticed a change. A receptionist greeted me, quickly told me they now worked by appointment only, and said it was now a ladies-only shop. She had just taken a significant slice off my thirty minutes.

Not to worry. I knew of at least three salons located in a large shopping mall on my way to the plant. Finding a parking space a short distance from the mall entrance, I proceeded to the information center. There were three salons in the mall to choose from, so I headed straight to the nearest one. I walked into the shop and was greeted with, "Please have a seat. I will be with you in about ten minutes." My first impression of the beautician wasn't good; she looked as though she had just survived a long night and left home in a really big hurry. I explained that I was in a hurry and would have to find another shop. I searched the mall for the other two shops but couldn't find either of them. At this point, the needle on my anxiety meter was reaching critical mass, all because my wife had insisted that I get a haircut before this important meeting.

I slowly came to the realization that the Holy Spirit must be involved in this. I sensed He was guiding me into something much more urgent than my meeting. It was an important meeting, one that included upper plant management and had taken considerable time and effort to schedule. I made the obvious decision; I would go to the meeting and skip the lesser important haircut. I headed for the parking lot, but for some unknown reason I suddenly had an overwhelming desire to get that haircut. The Holy Spirit made it abundantly clear; the meeting could wait, but the haircut could not. I was quickly losing control over what had begun as just another routine day. All my meticulous plans along with my allotted thirty minutes for a haircut had just gone up in smoke.

The Holy Spirit sent me back to the first shop I had found after leaving the information center. I walked in, and the young lady smiled and said, "Oh, you're back." I was a little puzzled because she wasn't at all surprised to see me. She spoke as if she knew I would be returning. She seated me, snapped the cape around my neck, and asked, "How would you like it cut?"

Sitting down, I began to feel the warmness of my Flame, the Holy Spirit, but I had no idea what was going to happen next. However, I quickly discovered this lady had a special place in our heavenly Father's heart. She had a very close personal relationship with Jesus. She had been praying about a need in her life; her prayers had been heard, and now God had me sitting in her barber chair, waiting to hear my next assignment. This was going to be an interesting day! I couldn't wait to hear her story. She was totally unaware of what was about to happen, but then so was I. I didn't know how, but I knew God was getting ready to change my landscape again. The Lord had sent me to provide the answer to her prayers. Here I was, seated in the midst of still another of God's plans for my life, totally clueless. All I knew was that our heavenly Father had taken notice of her situation and had sent me to help her through a very difficult season of her life.

My company owned a fleet of vehicles, most of which were small Ford Windstar vans. They were very nice and included all the accessories. When new vehicles were purchased, we then sold the older ones. There was one such vehicle that had recently become available to sell. My office manager advertised it in the sales section of the local newspaper. It would be a great family vehicle for a great price. Several people looked at it, but God chose not to allow any of them to purchase it. After a few weeks, I lowered the price, still with no success. I eventually came to the conclusion that we couldn't give it away, even if we tried. I wasn't aware of it, but God already had a special person in mind for that van.

Mona, the beautician who was about to give me a totally unforgettable haircut along with a lifelong memory, began the conversation by asking whether I preferred a scissors cut or a clippers cut. My response was, "Whichever is quickest, because I'm really in a big hurry." I was still concerned about getting to my all-important meeting on time.

The clippers buzzed. She was a great conversationalist, but mingled with the happy face she was wearing, I sensed some turbulent underlying currents of hopelessness and insurmountable problems. I also noticed she was very comfortable with the name of Jesus, since she mentioned Him often during the course of our conversation. I was excited to hear about her dependence on Christ and even more so when she told me she had accepted Him as her Lord and Savior many years ago. Mona hadn't yet shared her circumstances with me, but I knew they were coming. It was like the anticipation of waiting to start a new job. The Holy Spirit encouraged me to be patient, to sit and listen carefully. Her story would describe the job I was being given.

There was a lull in the conversation, so I took the liberty of asking whether she had family in town and which church she attended. As I waited for her answer, I sensed the Holy Spirit removing all the barriers between us. Then, totally unsolicited, she spent the next several minutes sharing her situation with me. She told her story with passion and emotion, as one would talk to a close friend.

She lived in an apartment with her two small children. Her husband, tired of his parental and marital responsibilities, had suddenly left his family without warning. She had been a stay-at-home mom, accustomed to caring for the kids and doing things moms do. Overnight she found herself thousands of miles from her family, alone with no job or source of income. Her husband had totally disappeared from the radar screen.

Although she had been educated as a beautician and had worked years earlier, her skills had become rusty since she had been out of her profession for quite some time. Her story was similar to many other single moms but without the urgency and severity of her circumstances. That day her story touched my heart in a way I shall never forget. While listening, I sensed the presence of Christ, the common link that bonded us together as brother and sister. My awareness of this spiritual relationship explained the necessity of my getting a haircut in that particular shop on that day.

She was a member of a great Christian church with a wonderful pastor. Her circle of friends at the church were very supportive and had provided the resources she needed to complete a cosmetology refresher course.

This certification would once again enable her to work as a beautician. Reestablishing herself in the profession, however, proved to be very difficult. She was successful in finding part-time employment, but it didn't pay enough to afford child care. Her car was no longer dependable, and she was broke. Her two-year-old was still in diapers, but she couldn't even afford to buy these essentials. The electricity had been turned off, and her apartment rent was past due. After several interviews, she had been hired on temp status by the owner of the beauty salon where I was now getting my much-needed haircut. On this morning, while on her way to work, her car engine had frozen up and left her stranded on the side of the road. The engine was beyond repair, so now she was also without transportation. A friend had picked her up and brought her to work, but now she had no way of getting home.

I sat quietly and listened. I found myself gazing into the face of a beautiful young mom who through no fault of her own had fallen headlong into the depths of poverty and despair. I also saw reflected in her eyes a healthy measure of hope and determination. She said she had asked Jesus many times, "Why are You letting this happen to me?" All the while knowing the answer that "all things work for the good of those who love the Lord" (Romans 8:28a). She looked forward with hope, knowing there was a silver lining somewhere behind this cloud of darkness. She shared these difficult moments of her personal life with me, and then looked at me with an expression that graciously said *Thank you for listening.* Her demeanor was proud and composed; she didn't ask me for help, but knowing I was in a hurry, she was very grateful that I had taken time to listen to her story.

She talked to me about her prayer life and assured me that she had prayed and cried until her eyes were dry—she had no tears left. During the course of our somewhat-one-sided conversation, God had given me a mental list of those things she needed most. In that moment I realized that, with the exception of one thing, God had already given me all the resources I needed to answer her prayers. I didn't know it, but He had been working out the details long before I walked into her shop. The Holy Spirit restated the simple fact: "It's not yours to give. It belongs to Me, and I Am that I Am is ready for you to part with it."

With that, I said to her, "The Lord has heard your prayers and has sent me by to deliver the things you requested." My Lord's logistics renders Amazon somewhere below elementary. Anyway, she knew her needs, but what she didn't know was what the Holy Spirit had told me to give her. I cannot explain the expression that came on her face, but I do believe if it hadn't been for gravity holding her down, she would have mistaken the moment for the rapture and ascended straight up to heaven. The saying "Her eyes were as big as saucers" seemed appropriate. I asked whether she could meet me when she got off from work. She said yes and told me she got off at two p.m. and would meet me in the mall food court.

I won't speculate on God's ability to compress or expand time, but I arrived at the plant and walked into the conference room for my all-important meeting with moments to spare. Amazing! We were awarded the project I had been praying for. Now I was concerned that some of the attendees would want to go out for lunch, as was often customary. I didn't have time for lunch since I had to be at the food court at two. God is so good; they excused themselves before I could even extend an invitation. They apologized and took a rain check. I then called my office manager and gave her a list of things to do in preparation for my meeting with Mona at two. By now she was accustomed to dealing with my sometimes-unusual requests.

I went to the office and picked up a large manila envelope, then drove to the mall. Again, incredibly I walked into the food court with a few moments to spare. Mona, with a surprised look, was waiting for me. Her expression came as no surprise, since only a few hours earlier, we had been complete strangers. She didn't know what to expect or even whether I would show up at all. Perhaps she was thinking *I will meet with this guy; I have nothing to lose.*

I sat down, smiled, and placed the envelope on top of the table in front of her. Her curiosity meter was maxed out, so I opened the envelope and took out the title to the van. The one I had been unable to sell. I gave it to her along with the keys and then explained that her vehicle was parked outside. It had been serviced, cleaned, and filled with gas. I also took a check from the envelope and gave it to her. It was more than adequate to cover insurance and other short-term expenses. There was another item on the tabletop, not in the envelope but in the form of a request. She had been asking God to give her a job with sufficient income to support her family. It was the one thing I couldn't give her, so I simply repeated to her what the Holy Spirit had told me. "God has heard your prayers and has answered them. He is going to give you a permanent and well-paying job." Other than when I asked my wife for her hand in marriage, I have never seen a more beautiful smile. I smiled back.

We sat and talked for a few more minutes, and during the conversation I noticed a hint of concern come over her face. She was young and attractive, and I'm sure she had been offered many things in return for less-than-honorable favors. As the conversation lulled, she looked at me and asked, "What do I have to give you in return for what you are doing for me?" I understood the reason behind her question and felt a little embarrassed. I honestly believe that had I asked for sexual favors in return, she would have said no and returned the gifts. Her guiding principles were well founded in Christ.

I smiled and told her that our heavenly Father didn't require payment for His favors, just obedience. She returned my smile as if she'd already known my answer; then together we offered a prayer of thanksgiving, giving Him all the honor and glory for providing for our every need. After taking care of the title transfer, I walked her to her new vehicle. She scrutinized its every detail, then rather giddily got in and drove away.

Four weeks passed, and the allotted time for my haircut once again rolled around. I made an appointment at my usual salon and made plans for the thirty minutes it would take. I walked in, and the receptionist greeted me; she told me the person who normally cut my hair was booked, but they had recently hired another beautician, who was really good. She asked whether I would consider using her instead. I said, "Sure, why not." I rounded the corner into the salon, and there stood Mona. She was standing in the center of God's blessings with a great, new full-time job and a beautiful smile.

I lost contact with her for a few years. Then one day, while at a restaurant having lunch with my wife, a strange lady ran up to me and for no apparent reason gave me an unexpected bear hug. You guessed it; it was Mona, and she was with her wonderful new husband, who just happened to be a youth minister.

My road to paradise had evolved from youthful indiscretion and unqualified decisions with no sense of direction into dependence on Christ as my resource for daily living. Once again, the landscape surrounding my road to paradise had changed. The ever-colorful and vibrant flowers Rose had planted along the way still flourished; the shoulders along my road were well tended, as evident by Joseph's loving care. Then there was Mona, sprinkling seeds of joy only a mother could sow along the way. She demonstrated the true meaning of faith, perseverance, and what it means to wait on the Lord. There is nothing more pleasant than walking out of the barber shop and experiencing a cool breeze as it dances around on one's neck. A refreshing haircut, a newfound friend, and the humbling experience of the Holy Spirit's guidance transformed a good day into a "triple-joy day."

I'm not sure of God's future plans for Mona, but if she is sitting at the table of the marriage supper of the Lamb when I arrive, perhaps she will greet me with, "I have been waiting to tell you that I have not cried, not even once, since the Lord brought me home to live with Him. Also, there are no more mortgages or utility bills to pay, no doctor visits or prescriptions to fill, no empty gas tanks or broken-down cars, no birthday parties or funerals to attend, and no weddings or marriages to celebrate. All this among millions of other wonderful blessings are now mine, all because I am the bride of the Son of God."

The Last Mile
Chapter 13

Given the opportunity, the last mile of one's journey suddenly becomes the most important and consuming of all life's endeavors. It is where life meets eternity. It often includes a journey into reminiscence, yet in reality it is the culmination of one's final walk through life. It is the prelude to one's final destination, the epitaph of the many choices made to reach that end. It looks back into the face of a multitude of neglected opportunities and what-ifs, things that perhaps should have been done differently. But in the final analysis, all these decisions, whether good, bad, or ugly, will be blended together and used to cast the mold for the key that unlocks one of two gates that open into eternity.

These, along with a variety of other reasons, can make the last mile of one's journey the most difficult, emotional, and expensive portion of his or her entire road of life. It is a time when everyone comes face-to-face with reality; for many, it is the most heart-wrenching time they will ever encounter. The last mile culminates in one of two eternal destinations; either the best is yet to come, or the worst is yet to come. These represent an unavoidable and irreversible encounter with eternity that may come suddenly, without warning, or may extend into months or even years. Regardless of the circumstances or choices we have made, life will eventually complete its course, and all these concerns will become self-evident.

As a child of God, "the best is yet to come" describes the journey along my road to paradise. However, along the way I have encountered many people who were unprepared for the last mile of their earthly journey. Sadly, these will be condemned by their own choices, because for them the worst is yet to come. Each of these scenarios illustrates approaching the completion of one's life on earth; from an individual and very personal perspective, they look forward into eternity and their final destination. They also with absolute certainty will reap the consequences of the lifestyle they had chosen to live, a life of obedience to Christ or Satan and the enticements of this world. This decision and the consequences that follow will serve as the steering mechanisms that guide your course through life, eventually bringing you to the gates of eternity.

Gates is another one of those versatile words that can be used to enrich our understanding of a variety of subjects, both physical and spiritual. In a physical sense the word is generally used to illustrate nothing more than a simple structure used to allow entrance or exit, to keep something in from getting out—or vice versa, to keep something out from getting in. But spiritually gates depict two ways of life—gates that open to two roads: one leading to everlasting life in Christ and the other leading to Satan and eternal destruction. These two gates illustrate the reality of our life choices, which grow larger and larger as we approach the last step of our last mile. Time waits for no one. "Enter through the narrow gate. For wide is the gate and broad is the road that leads to destruction, and many enter through it. But small is the gate and narrow the road that leads to life, and only a few find it" (Matthew 7:13–14).

Whether accepted or rejected, Pascal's Wager provides the perfect backdrop for the two gates depicted in Matthew. Consciously or not, we are all in pursuit of a final answer to his famous wager, which becomes self-evident in the end. Again, the question begs for an answer. "Does God really exists or have I made the terrible and irreversible mistake of believing He doesn't exist?" If while looking back you are reminded of how you stubbornly denied God's existence, you now find yourself standing before the Son of God, who holds the keys to the gates of both heaven and hell.

On our last vacation, my wife and I visited Carlsbad Caverns National Park in New Mexico. We hiked from the natural entrance down to the Big Room, which by the way was very big. From there we took a one-and-a-half-hour ranger-guided tour through several named "rooms" in the cave, culminating in the spectacular King's Palace. Along the way we stopped in the Queen's Room, where our guide demonstrated to the group the experience of total darkness. We were about eight hundred feet below the surface of the earth when the ranger said, "Lights out, and please, no noise." With that he turned off all the lights. They remained off for about three minutes, although it seemed much longer.

There was something about experiencing this degree of total darkness and not being able to see, hear, or touch anything that quickly became very unsettling. I had never experienced solitude or darkness to that degree before. While sitting in this dark, silent cave, my thoughts turned to being separated from God and being cast into total darkness for eternity. It was a horrible thought and one we on earth can never experience, not even in the depths of a dark cave. It also brought reality to the statement "The worst is yet to come," which means total separation from God. The seven "I Am" statements Christ made in the book of John open the door to a relationship with Him; inversely, they can also give us some insight of what we will experience throughout eternity in the absence of a relationship with Jesus, resulting in total separation from God.

The Son of God said, "I Am the Light of the world." *Since you rejected Christ on earth, you will now live without recourse in utter darkness throughout eternity.*

"I Am the Door." *You refused to come into My Father's kingdom on earth, and now the gate to heaven is permanently closed to you. Your key doesn't fit.*

"I Am the Bread of Life." *You wouldn't accept Christ as your Savior while on earth. Now you will hunger forever for the Bread of Life without satisfaction.*

"I Am the Good Shepherd." *My sheep heard my voice on earth and followed Me, but you refused to listen, and now you will never hear the Shepherd call again, because you are separated from Him as far as the east is from the west.*

"I Am the Resurrection." *I was crucified for your sins, resurrected to give you the gift of eternal life in heaven with Me, but you chose Satan and his world instead; now you will live in torment with him forever. I won't die for you again.*

"I Am the Way." *I am a way of life that leads to life everlasting. You chose a way of life that leads to death. The road that leads to paradise is closed forever to you.*

Because you have rejected Christ on earth, you have now been separated from God the Father. You will never again experience the Father's love, goodness, and mercy. You shall no longer have the opportunity to be sheltered beneath the umbrella of God's grace. Your cries of anguish cannot be heard because you are separated from God by a great gulf that no one can cross. God is love, but you are now separated forever from His love and destined to live eternally with Satan.

With your last mile behind, your key unlocks the wide gate that you will now pass through and into eternity with hell as your new and permanent home. It is a place deafened by the sounds of gnashing teeth and total darkness. The mind of mortal man cannot comprehend the slightest meaning of what it means to be separated from God. Hell is often described as God's garbage dump; everything unfit for heaven will be thrown in and tormented by its fires. Because of the symbolic nature of the language, some people question whether hell consists of actual fire. Such reasoning will bring no comfort to those who are living in sin, but the horribleness of its reality will be far greater than we can imagine. The Bible exhausts human language in describing heaven and hell. "The former is more glorious, and the latter more terrible, than language can express."[6]

The good news is that the gate to hell can be forever closed and replaced with the love, joy, and peace that come through a personal relationship with the Son of God. He holds your key to paradise; He has already walked that last mile and prepared your final destination. It is just a simple matter of trusting in God's plan for your life, a plan that transitions from a carnal nature into the spiritual nature of Christ as your Savior.

It began a long time ago when God imposed time on Adam and Eve by opening the gates to the Garden of Eden. When the gates opened, they were expelled from the garden, and the gates closed behind them. This closed garden gate symbolizes the same gate that now through Jesus Christ stands open wide between our Father's earthly kingdom and His heavenly kingdom. Remember, Christ said, "I am the door." The gate is symbolic, yet it emerges into reality through Christ when the final step of one's last mile is completed.

Picture the image of our Redeemer, God's Son, as He steps over the threshold of the gates of heaven, stopping to gaze through time down that long road to Calvary—a road no mortal man could have traveled, one that would end in humiliation, suffering, crucifixion, and death. He endured these sacrifices for our sake. He walked the last mile of His journey on earth and paid the price with His life, the bride's price. He was crucified for the sole purpose of our redemption. As the Son of God and then by virtue of His resurrection, He now holds the keys to these two most profound and unique of all gates, the gates to eternity, both heaven and hell. There is a small gate that opens to a narrow road leading back to heaven, the Garden of Eden, the holy hills of heaven and paradise. There is also a large gate that opens to a broad road leading to hell and eternal damnation. These

---

[6] Nelson's Illustrated Bible Dictionary, *Hell* (Thomas Nelson Publisher, New York-Camden-Nashville 1986), p. 473.

two gates represent the most important gates the world will ever experience. They materialized from the mind of God and emerged into the real world when Christ left behind an empty cross and walked away from His burial place, leaving behind a vacant tomb with the burial wrappings still in place.

The Lamb of God, Christ, stands where the roads of life end and eternity begins. In His hands rests a book, the Book of Life. Those names found written in the Lamb's Book of Life are the ones who have accepted the Father's proposal to become the bride of Christ. Those who rejected His proposal to become His Son's bride aren't invited to the marriage supper of the Lamb; their names aren't found written in the Book of Life. Standing by the gates, the Son of God scans the pages of the Book of Life in search of names. One by one moms, dads, brothers, sisters, relatives, and friends stand before Him. He looks into the horrified faces of those who have rejected Him and says, "Depart from me, go and serve the one you served while on earth; I never knew you." Your name is not found in His Book of Life. Your last mile now lies behind you and your final destination ahead—total separation from God throughout eternity.

The gates of the Garden of Eden protect the Tree of Life from the world, although the door is open through Jesus Christ. These gates chaperon eternity, sheltering it from time and defending paradise against the sinful world in which humanity lives. God's Son is the only one who can open that gate; He is the key, and there are no duplicates. It is this key that closes the gate to hell and opens the gate to heaven, or sadly, opens the gate to hell and closes the gate to heaven.

What I thought was my last mile approached suddenly and without warning. I'm not sure, given the circumstances, that I was mentally capable of making a conscious choice or decision at that time. Fortunately I had already chosen the small gate and narrow road that led to the Tree of Life many years before. My reality check began about three months earlier while sitting in church one Sunday morning. I was sitting next to the aisle along the wall of the sanctuary. While the pastor was speaking, I felt a presence on my left side. I looked over and saw an opaque, barely visible image of what appeared to be an outstretched arm. It was draped in a heavy robe with its hand extended toward me. My hair stood up; I knew it was the Holy Spirit. I quickly looked away, not knowing what to expect. I looked again, and the image was still there. I reached out to take His hand, and the Holy Spirit said to me, "No matter what happens, I will be with you." I was frightened;

my immediate thoughts turned to my wife, children, and close friends. I was concerned that something really bad was going to happen to one of them.

Several weeks went by without incident; then early one morning, my world turned upside down. I have an exercise room in my home and often got up early to work out. It was about seven o'clock on this particular Sunday morning, and after working out, I left my exercise room to shower and get dressed for church. While on my way to shower, I began to feel really weird. I took an aspirin and checked my blood pressure, which was normally in the range of 124 over 70; but it was very high—stroke level. I was very active and had always enjoyed exceptionally good health, so I dismissed these early warning signs as overexertion in my workout routine. I headed for the shower again, thinking that a hot shower would clear everything up.

At that point I began to experience an unusual pain in my chest; I didn't make it to the shower. The pain intensified, and my blood pressure became very erratic. Then the elephant came and sat down on my chest; I then realized I was having a heart attack. I don't know how a four-thousand-pound elephant managed to get into my house and sit on my chest, but it did. I told my wife I was feeling bad and asked her to take me to the hospital emergency room; I was afraid to tell her I was having a heart attack. I sat down and waited while she brought me a pair of jogging pants and a shirt. By this time I was experiencing excruciating pain and had become drenched with sweat. I looked at my beautiful wife of thirty years for what I expected would be the last time. Then again, with what I thought were my last words, I said to her, "Call an ambulance; I'm having a heart attack." Without warning, what appeared to be my last mile lay behind and my final destination loomed before me.

It is most likely difficult for many of you to understand or appreciate this next statement, but while sitting in that chair in excruciating pain, waiting for the ambulance to arrive, I experienced unimaginable joy and peace. It was a warm and comfortable sensation that overshadowed and absorbed the severe pain my body was experiencing. While sitting there, I visualized my arm outstretched toward a door that opened into heaven. I knew that within a few moments, I would be going home to live with the Son of God. The prospect was exciting beyond words. I knew He was standing on the other side, waiting for me, but regardless of my best efforts, I couldn't stretch out my arm far enough to grasp that door handle. I wasn't allowed to open it.

Later that day while in cardiac ICU, I overheard the doctor tell my wife, "If he makes it through the next twenty-four hours, his chance of surviving will hopefully improve." Later that morning, my Flame, the Holy Spirit, placed a mental que card directly in front of me, which read, "I told you I would be with you no matter what happens." That warm sensation I had felt so many times before and then again in the midst of the pain of the heart attack visited me again; it was my Comforter. He held my hand and walked with me through a myocardial infarction of the left descending ventricle, commonly known as the "widow maker."

While I was sitting in the chair, waiting for the paramedics to arrive, my faith and hope came face-to-face with the reality of eternity. I had almost walked the last mile of my road to paradise but wasn't given the privilege of completing my journey. Although my Lord didn't unlock the gate, my brush with death was the most exciting and wonderful thing that ever happened in my life. It was, in every respect, truly a miracle—not in the sense that I had survived but rather that I had come within moments of actually seeing the face of the Son of God. My faith and hope, which had brought me to that point, vanished into the absolute assurance that yes, He is real. I no longer had faith and hope in things unseen; and although I didn't see the face of my Savior that day, the Holy Spirit proved to me beyond doubt the reality of the person of Christ. The spiritual significance of the statement "The best is yet to come" unfolded before my eyes. As a result of the heart attack, I had just experienced a series of the most enlightening and best days of my entire life; all were underscored by the love, joy, and peace that came from my Lord and Savior. I now understood that when living in the joy of Christ, all days are good.

My portrayal of the worst is yet to come—total separation from God— was derived from the antonyms of John's "I Am" statements. Now let's look at the positive impact of those "I Am" statements within the context of "the best is yet to come." My journey on earth would continue with no idea of Father's plans for my future, but regardless of where my road to paradise led, I would go with the total assurance that the Holy Spirit would be walking with me, hand in hand every step of the way. I am also absolutely sure of three things: The remaining portion of my road to paradise will be filled with opportunities, challenges, and excitement; and only He knows the time and place I will walk my last mile. Finally, I know beyond a doubt that the best *is* yet to come.

Christ is truly the door that opens to my future new home and address, the holy hills of heaven and the end of *My Road to Paradise*. As the bride of

Christ I will one day live in the presence of My Father throughout eternity. In my new home there will be no darkness since the glory of God and the Lamb will illuminate the landscapes of heaven. The Light of the World that was rejected will now shine on paradise throughout eternity. There will be no marriages in heaven. I will have a new body, and neither will there be any more sickness, pain, sorrow, death, or crying. I will leave all of these things behind, for they will have all passed away. I will transition from faith and hope of an eternal home in heaven to knowing that a way of life in Christ while on earth has now led me to life eternal with Jesus.

I have found it to be both challenging and amazing how God selects us to help others in their time of need. It is a gratifying experience since blessings flow equally to both the giver and the receiver. Within this context, the Holy Spirit, with what amounted to nothing more than a fleeting thought, asked me, "Do you now understand what it means for Me to take hold of your hand and guide you through life?" My immediate answer was yes. He responded, "No, you do not." He explained, "Yes, while helping someone in need, you are both blessed, but it is not always about either the helping hand or the receiver of the gift. I sent Rose, Joseph, and Mona along with many others into your life to test your faith and obedience. I placed them in your life as helpers to take hold of your hand (not for you to take hold of their hands as you have thought) to guide you along your road to paradise. They were my servants, and I employed the circumstances of their lives to serve as guideposts along your way. I placed them there to mark the boundaries of your road to paradise."

Now as I look into the bowls of those two red wine glasses and reflect on an occasional haircut, I see a road that isn't built on the material things of this life. Instead I see the reflection of a road shaped by intertwined and complex relationships with others and clearly marked by the Holy Spirit of the Father and Son.

I searched for my road to paradise and found it hidden in the joy of Jesus Christ. I discovered that paradise wasn't just about dreams that were gathered around the pleasures of this world; rather it was hidden in the reality of *knowing the best is yet to come.* So I continue on my journey, but I now go with a new and different perspective of the time of my life that remains.

Epilogue

The table of contents of *My Road to Paradise* is more than just a list of chapters. It defines the progression of how wonderful our lives can be from the concept of "The Family Circle" through "The Last Mile" of our life and its final destination—eternity. "The Family Circle" is centered on our heavenly Father's love for us and in like manner parent's love for their own children. It pursues maturity in this earthly home with our family comfortably seated around "The Table." From there, a Christ-centered foundation is laid, which enables every sibling to travel "The Road of Life" of his or her own choosing. It leads us through periods of failure, hardship, and disappointments; but along the way, we will also experience success, love, and happiness, all underwritten with the joy of a Christ-centered life.

"The Blender" is pictured as taking all our life experiences and blending them together with "The Bible," our new playbook, which introduces us to "The Father," "The Son," and "The Holy Spirit." The blended ingredients produce the perfect mixture, which conforms to the plans God has for our lives, plans that will often stretch the meaning of the words *faith* and *hope* but we will know that through it all the Holy Spirit will walk hand in hand with us through "The Last Mile" of this earthly journey. Given the opportunity as we approach our final destination, we will be confronted with the reality of either knowing the best is yet to come or being horrified with the image of the worst yet to come.

It is our heavenly Father's desire that no man, woman, or child be left behind. Everyone needs to be brought to the saving knowledge of Jesus Christ; it would be a terrible mistake to deny Christ and waste a life solely on the pleasures of this world. What will we have gained if we owned the whole world but lost our eternal souls, and even more horrifying, those entrusted to our guidance? After walking "The Last Mile," what will we have gained if we discover we have lost everything and that the worst is still yet to come? Life doesn't have to end this way, since faith in God and His Son is enough to ensure you that yes, the best awaits you at the end of your road to paradise, where "The Family Circle" of God awaits your arrival. Your new address can be:

A Child of God
C/O The Holy Hills of Heaven

Welcome home to paradise.

Printed in the United States
By Bookmasters